Invitations to the World

Teaching and Writing for the Young

Richard Peck

portions of this book
previously published as
Love and Death at the Mall

DIAL BOOKS
NEW YORK

Published by Dial Books
A division of Penguin Putnam Inc.
345 Hudson Street
New York, New York 10014

Designed by Lily Malcom
Text set in Garamond 3
Printed in the U.S.A. on acid-free paper
1 3 5 7 9 10 8 6 4 2

Library of Congress Cataloging-in-Publication Data
Peck, Richard, date.
Invitations to the world : teaching and
writing for the young / Richard Peck.
p. cm.
Rev. ed. of: Love and death at the mall. New York : Delacorte Press, © 1994.
Includes bibliographical references.
ISBN 0-8037-2734-8
1. Peck, Richard, date. 2. Authors, American—20th century—Biography.
3. Teachers—United States—Biography. 4. Peck, Richard, date—Authorship.
5. Young adult fiction—Authorship. 6. Young adults—Books and reading.
I. Peck, Richard, date. Love and death at the mall. II. Title.
PS3566.E2526 Z473 2002
818'.5409—dc21
(B)   2001053691

Dedicated to Sheldon Fogelman

INVITATIONS
TO THE WORLD

It seems to me that people who advise "write what you know" drastically underestimate the human capacity for imagining what lies beyond our immediate knowledge and for understanding what is new to us. Equally, they overestimate the extent to which we know ourselves.

— Ann Cameron,
"Write What You Care About,"
School Library Journal, June 1989

This is a book about reading and writing and young people, and about writing for young people who read. It organizes itself around the questions that follow writers wherever we go:

But how did you get your start?
And where do you get your ideas?

Then that third question that begins to crop up as your career ripens:

So how much longer are you going to write?

These are the three perennially most popular questions because they don't require the reading of a line we ever wrote.

I'm a writer because I was once a teacher in America in a time when teachers were becoming the only adults in the daily lives of teenage students.

I learned to be a teacher as I was to learn to be a writer, where I was already on the job, the only adult in the room, and the door was closed between me and all help. In teaching I thought I'd found my true calling because it made me laugh and cry and kept me up at night. Like writing.

But How Did You Get Your Start?

Well, how did we? M. E. Kerr says she had stationery printed up and then submitted her first works through her own phantom literary agency. John Updike walked directly from Harvard graduation into his writing room and is still in there. Françoise Sagan, S. E. Hinton, Truman Capote, Gore Vidal all published shortly after puberty and were being lionized when they were still cubs. Spared all this precocity, I never wrote a line of fiction until I was thirty-seven years old, and even then only because I'd been driven to this extreme by seventh-graders.

CHAPTER ONE

"We read to know we're not alone."
C. S. Lewis

I suspect we all began early in childhood. Whatever is going to become of us, we speak our first words as we're taking our first steps. For some of us, embryonic writers, those first steps are on the road to readers.

This isn't to say that people can't be taught to write, and to write better. But nobody but a reader ever became a writer. Even the authors who pass themselves off as natural phenomena, and who were much misunderstood at school, appear to have a stronger grasp on paragraph development and vocabulary than the national norm. Becoming a writer involves extended study and more practice than the piano or football: models, revision as a religion, and that best of teaching tools and foreshadowing of an adult future—the wholesome fear of an F.

But some of us were surely becoming writers before we could read, well before we ever saw school.

For a start, my mother read to me before I could read for myself. A satisfactory substitute for that technique has yet to be devised. She wouldn't teach me to read, but being there on her lap, watching the page and hearing stories over again, must have been what is now called "prereading experience." My mother wasn't trying to make me a published writer. She was trying to make me a successful first-grader when I got there. Because she intoxicated me with words, I entered grade school with a vocabulary I can't find in the letters ninth-graders send to me now. She opened the door to the alternative world of books, and the minute I looked through it, I saw more interesting lives than mine. And I still do.

She taught me how to print the letters of the alphabet, though not the spelling of words. I had to know the letters in order to conduct a correspondence. For every gift from a grandparent, I was to write a letter of thanks in response. The intended lesson here might have been gratitude rather than composition. But, anyway, I had a table and chair, my size, along the kitchen wall. From her station at the sink my mother suggested phrasing and ghostwrote, telling me how to spell out the words and leave spaces between. We included punctuation. At the age of four and five I was taking dictation and conducting a correspondence. Strange? Not as far as I knew.

Would I rather have been belly-flopping on a Flexible Flyer

down the steepest hill in Fairview Park? Maybe, but in an everyday way my mother forged the link between reading and writing before I could actually do either. Fortunately she got to me well ahead of the secondary-school English classes that present "units" in literature, composition, grammar, and even prose and poetry as separate and unrelated subjects. I suppose her approach was "whole language" ahead of its time.

From the Brothers Grimm onward, the stories my mother and I had read were of the long ago and far away. Far from failing to relate, I valued them for that remoteness. In books it seemed you could go anywhere and conquer time. They readied me for a writer I was to meet somewhat later, a staple for boys then, though he's largely forgotten now. He was an American gentleman-adventurer named Richard Halliburton. The prototype of Indiana Jones, he was always on the Royal Road to somewhere: the Taj Mahal, the Valley of the Kings, the South China Sea, where he in fact disappeared.

We learned multiculturalism from Richard Halliburton. He had the gift to reveal exotic cultures as if we were standing beside him, seeing for ourselves. Without spelling it out he indicated that Christian Caucasian English-speakers were in a distinct minority if you took a global view. He was no Englishman surveying his empire from above; he was the last gasp of the American Richard Harding Davis tradition, reporting from the wide world before the winds of World War II blew it away.

Richard Halliburton led us out of the early childhood world of Teutonic gnomes and British nursery rhymes and those worrisome trolls under that bridge. It appeared that you could escape into reality, and another link was forged. This one was between Halliburton's globe-trotting and the monthly arrival of *National Geographic* and that heart-stopping map that fell out of each issue like an invitation. Stories and maps and the promise of escape in both fused.

Then, when we got to school, it was the era when geography was still being taught. There were maps here too, big ones. And there like a banner across the top of the blackboard was the whole alphabet, written out in Palmer Method, caps and lowercase. The world unfurled before us. But we were six by then, and that's late in life. Most of what we'll be is already decided before we ever see school. Formal education doesn't build foundations; it builds upon them.

I hadn't spent my whole preschool life curled up with a good book or conducting a correspondence. Far from it. There was kindergarten, which was private then. You paid tuition and went to Miss Howe's in a big old house with pocket doors that had seen better days. Our mothers thought well of kindergarten because in this first socializing we could give one another the childhood diseases of that time—chicken pox, measles, whooping cough—and get them behind us before the academics of first grade. It wasn't just measles either. It was German measles, which had a far more ominous ring.

In the middle of the morning at Miss Howe's we pushed back from our activities and marched around the room to burn off excess energy. The piano accompaniment was by Miss Beth Butts. She must have played by ear, because each day she asked a different child to choose a marching song. Then she went right into it, rendering anything in march time. I don't remember what anybody else chose. Given the time, it might have been "Deep Purple." When my turn came, I chose "Sidewalks of New York."

She gave that old chestnut the kind of double take a child always notices in an adult. "Why do you want that song?" Miss Butts inquired.

"Because I'll be moving to New York."

"Really?" She knew my parents well and how firmly rooted they were. "Soon?"

"Well, as soon as I can get there," I said. We marched that morning around Miss Howe's to "Sidewalks of New York," Miss Butts grinning wildly to herself at the keyboard and I trying to feel the pavement of a real city beneath my feet.

S. E. Hinton, who hadn't been born yet, was to say that there are people who go and people who stay. Writers tend to be the former, always nagged by the notion we should be somewhere else, that wherever we are, the party isn't. I recall that kindergarten morning after more than sixty years, here at a desk, my size, in a room lined with books, in New York.

Twenty Minutes a Day

Read to your children
Twenty minutes a day;
You have the time,
And so do they.

Read while the laundry is in the machine;
Read while the dinner cooks;
Tuck a child in the crook of your arm
And reach for the library books.

Hide the remote,
Let the computer games cool,
For one day your children will be off to school;
"Remedial"? "Gifted"? You have the choice;
Let them hear their first tales
In the sound of your voice.

Read in the morning;
Read over noon;
Read by the light of
Goodnight Moon.

Turn the pages together,
Sitting close as you'll fit,
Till a small voice beside you says,
"Hey, don't quit."

CHAPTER TWO

When I finally got around to being a writer, my childhood was dimmer in my mind than it is now, thirty years later. I was living a thousand miles from home, and the world had turned upside down several times: three wars and five presidents, television, the power shifts of the 1960's, the divorce rate that had spiked like a fever chart. And for more than a decade I'd been a teacher, convinced that the whole process of growing up, going to school, coming of age had changed beyond all recognition. I'd spent my whole youth waiting for the freedoms my thirteen-year-old students already had. And I'd been spared much they had to face.

Those students weren't interested in my reminiscences, as any teacher learns. Any attempt to replay for them coming of age in the Golden 1950's, a time made safer by diagramed sentences, met with a poor review. They'd heard all these tales from their parents, and they didn't believe them. The young themselves warned me well in advance that a novel had better never be the autobiography of the author. It had far better be the biography of the person the reader would like to be.

At every age people read fiction for the shock of recognition, and so I began a career writing in the present, for and about a generation I never was.

Only in the fifth book did the old days come back to me. Nostalgia, maybe, and the urge to share something of the past with a generation robbed of it by suburbia and the decline of history as a school subject.

I thought, too, that if I remained locked into the present with my readers, I'd burn out of writing, as I'd just done as a teacher. Besides, a lot of good American writing looks back, often in the child's view of elders, as in this snippet from Florence King:

> To make sure I learned the etiquette of grieving, Granny took me with her to the many funerals she attended. O Death, where is thy Sting? Search me. I grew up looking at so many corpses that I still feel a faint touch of surprise whenever I see people move.[1]

I had elders of my own, and the first loves of my life had been local and family history. It had something to do with being born at the nadir of the Great Depression: that belief that I'd

1. *Reflections in a Jaundiced Eye,* St. Martin's Press, 1989.

been born after the party was over. The tree-arched brick streets of old houses in our town. Victorian hulks with turrets behind deep porches. The young Abraham Lincoln rendered in bronze and holding an ax on the courthouse steps, and emblazoned beneath:

AT TWENTY-ONE I CAME TO ILLINOIS

All the stories my mother read were from the past, and so were all the readings to come in school and college curricula. I made the connection early between the glamour of the past on the page and the living history of the town around me.

All fiction writing depends on the amassing of a lunatic amount of observed material. I was gathering material long before I knew what to do with it. Writers and children are natural snoops, though writers call it "research." Had I known how brief childhood is, I'd have looked closer.

Even before that fifth book, I was bootlegging bits of the past in my novels about the present. As early as the second, *Dreamland Lake,* a once-notable character in my hometown turns up in a contemporary novel. In the book she's a reclusive old woman living on Flip and Brian's paper route, Old Lady Garrison.

In fact she'd been Mrs. Baldwin, a living landmark of Decatur, Illinois. Even her house was famous, but since its story predates hers, I won't spill it here in the hope I can use it later. We watched Mrs. Baldwin being chauffeur-driven slowly through the streets in a magnificent LaSalle automobile with white sidewalls. She was our own Queen Mary and dressed like her, circa 1910. We never glimpsed her face because she was heavily veiled, and dressed in all weathers in unrelieved white.

The story grown up around her was that at the turn of the century her small son had darted out into West Main Street to be struck down by a dairy van. As he lay dying he said, "Mother, always wear white so I can see you."

She always did, decades after his untimely death. This story sounds enough like a myth to be the truth. As a future novelist I was willing to blend the two. But fiction isn't real life written down. In real life I never went near Mrs. Baldwin. Perhaps because of that, the boys in *Dreamland Lake* meet her face-to-face:

> She reached out a claw and took it, holding it up so we could see it. It was a picture of a boy, sitting on a bench with one leg crossed under him. He was in short pants, maybe ten or eleven years old. "This is the best portrait of him that I have," she explained. "Though he was in his first pair of long pants when I lost him. He was my son, Oliver Hatfield Garrison, the only child I had. If he had been spared to me, he would have been a Circuit Court Judge, possibly a State Senator today."

The generation gap is briefly spanned and contact made. In books we want what real life withholds. We write not the scene we played, but the one we didn't.

Even in Mrs. Baldwin's cameo role as Old Lady Garrison, I faced a problem that would recur. Real-life people don't fit into fiction until they've been edited out of all semblance of themselves. Fiction can never be real life with the names changed. Real life is too coincidental, melodramatic, diffuse, badly timed. Real people are too extreme for fiction. "Stranger than fiction," we say. "You wouldn't believe it if you read it in a book." How true.

Uncle Miles in the fifth book, *The Ghost Belonged to Me,* proved that. When I decided to set a story entirely in the past, it was to be about my hometown in the early twentieth century as recalled by my great-uncle Miles Peck.

In a town full of old characters and aggressive eccentrics, my great-uncle reigned supreme. He would have been a contemporary of Mrs. Baldwin, but he got around more. At eighty-five Uncle Miles worked when he wanted to, fished when he wanted to, and said rude things in front of people's mothers. I thought he was God. Grown-ups dreaded him, and so I was his last listener, dazed as with drink on his stories of all the old scandals of the town.

He was a carpenter who drove a Model A Ford fitted out with a carpentry box where the rumble seat had been, and he used his trade chiefly as a way of invading people's privacy. He trundled around the town collecting new stories and delivering others, some of them seventy years out of date. Though he wouldn't have read fiction, from him I may have learned that a novel is gossip trying to pass as art. In any case, he was the old man I wanted to be one day, and became.

Long after he was dead I wanted Uncle Miles back. For me he embodied the storytelling tradition. All history is local history. All stories are family stories. Every tale must sound as if it's being spoken aloud, overheard. But before he became the fictional Uncle Miles Armsworth, I had unforeseen difficulties in changing him. His language, for one thing. And though for purposes of the novel he appears to be an old bachelor, in real life he'd married often, though never seriously.

More importantly, in the novel he had to have a warmly human relationship with his young great-nephew. In real life my uncle Miles barely noticed me, and addressed me, if at all, absentmindedly by my father's name. Too many generations had gotten by Uncle Miles, who was far more interested in the story than the listener.

In *The Ghost Belonged to Me* a boy who isn't me closely allies with his great-uncle. They have mutual adventures, their bond is briefly intense, as one is just entering the world and the other is just leaving. Stories aren't real life. They're comments upon real life, parallel universes of what might be if our ties were stronger and the world a more coherent place.

But what of that title with "The Ghost" in it? My own uncle Miles never told ghost stories. Real life was enough for him without drawing in the supernatural, and enough for me too.

Still, as I worked on the novel, letters were coming from young readers of my four earlier books. The boys wrote back, "Why don't you write about the weird? Ever heard of Stephen King?" A direct quote: "Can't find a thing you've written on the Bermuda Triangle."

I'd been trying to write responsible, reasonably realistic novels of modern life. I'd wanted to hold up a mirror to my readers. I'd thought they wanted to be recognized by books. They did, but they wanted to see themselves in more interesting (less seriously challenging) settings. They wanted characters that reminded them of themselves in fantasy; sagas of the unexplained; *Star Wars-Robocop*-cyberpunk science fiction; time travel; and above all, according to the letters, ghost stories.

I held out, though I was being given more authoritative guidance than any book reviewer's. The story I was writing was strong on action anyway and too long on nostalgia. Bowing to the letters, I introduced a ghost into the proceedings, which meant starting over from word one.

The minute this dead girl entered, the book came alive. Now I was a long way from the initial inspiration for the story: my great-uncle, his memories of our hometown. But I was moving steadily to one more unexpected event in a career full of them. Walt Disney Productions was waiting with a television contract on the day the book was published, a contract that wouldn't have been forthcoming without the ghost in the story. I vowed to read the mail from young readers with hawk eyes for all the clues they could give about where my books should go from here.

But we were talking about Uncle Miles and how different a book character has to be from his real-life inspiration, and how far fiction inevitably is from fact and recall. In the novel Uncle Miles has to be a believer in the supernatural, with evidence he considers convincing. And he has to be much closer to his great-nephew, Alexander, than my uncle Miles ever drew to me. Here's a scene from the book, a story within the story:

"You believe in ghosts, Uncle Miles?"

"What brought that to mind all of a sudden?" He laid down his hammer and took a plug of tobacco.

"Oh—I was reading a book—a library book—of ghost stories, and I just wondered if you maybe had an opinion."

Uncle Miles took two nails out of his mouth to make room for the plug. "Well, I am no hand at reading," he said, settling back. "But I don't hold with written-down ghost stories anyhow. They leave a person with the idee you have to have castles and dungeons and like that to attract a ghost. A lot of them stories are German anyway, so you got to take that into account. Some of them is English too. So you want to take into consideration that they're the products of two pooped-out peoples."

He worked his jaws in silence for a while. I knew the day's work was at an end. "No," he said, "I wouldn't put any stock in made-up stories, especially them that claim to have took place in ancient days gone by. But of course there is ghosts."

It was evening then, and the katydids were starting up their whine in the Dutch elm. And the barn towered over us. Nothing moved but Uncle Miles's jaw as he chewed.

"Naw," I told him. "There aren't such things as ghosts."

"Don't say what you don't know. I bunked in with a feller who seen one to his sorrow."

"Naw," I said hopefully.

"Boy, I don't lie."

Then he told me the story.

"Oh, it was twenty years ago and being restless I took off for the southern part of the state. Had a job down there at Teutopolis as drayman for the Star Store. I was weary of carpentry for a time and wanted a change.

"At the boarding house was a feller name of Cleatus Watts. He'd lost his best friend during an epidemic of the swamp fever which could be very bad down there at the time. People dropped like flies, laid in a coma, and flickered out.

"Anyhow, they'd buried Cleatus's friend a month before I come to town. And one time Cleatus come back to his room late. And there stood his friend in the room, facing away from the door. Why, for a minute it seemed so natural that Cleatus forgot the feller was dead. When he got his wits about him, he was in the room alone.

"He come down the hall and told me about it, and I said he was being fanciful.

"Well, the next night it was the same story. Cleatus come into his room, and there the ghost of his departed friend stood, facing away from Cleatus and in a great anguish. The ghost was as real as the living man, Cleatus said. And it was tearing its hair and clawing the air something pitiful.

"Cleatus hotfooted it down to my room again, but when we went back, the ghost was gone, though the room smelled something wicked. Cleatus said that this sort of thing was getting on his nerves and did I think we ought to take lodgings elsewhere.

"I told him no, since the ghost of his friend was appearing to him for some purpose and would likely follow wherever he went. Cleatus took no comfort in this but saw the sense of it.

"Well, sir, third night running the ghost returned. And I tell you, I heard it myself. I was in bed but awake and heard Cleatus go into his room. There was quiet then, but I smelled graves.

"Then a voice I never heard before echoed down that hallway like a bell pealing. 'Turn me over, Cleatus!' It said. I can hear it yet. 'IN GOD'S NAME, TURN ME OVER!'"

"Cleatus come pounding down the hall, half wild. But I stepped out and told him I'd heard it too, which was some relief to him. Why, that voice raised everybody in the place. There was a head poked out of every door and witnesses a-plenty.

"'But what can he mean?' Cleatus says to me, grabbing hold of my arm like a child. 'What does TURN ME OVER signify?'

"I didn't know the answer to that one. But a bunch of us in the boarding house lit a lamp and went downstairs to put our heads together. The landlady set in with us, very concerned that her place might develop a bad name.

"It was her idee to take this problem to another woman who lived down there right outside of town. She sold herbs and root-mixtures and was otherwise a woman of wisdom. So that night Cleatus slept on the floor of my room, and the next day all of us paid this woman a call, a very dried-up old party but highly respected.

"She heard us out and nodded like she knowed where to put her finger on the problem. 'Get an affidavit from the county coroner,' she said, 'and have your friend's grave dug up and opened.'

"Some of us didn't like the sound of that and didn't see the point to it, but Cleatus was takin' the whole thing so bad we thought it couldn't hurt.

"Well, the coroner was under the influence of this wise woman anyway and oversaw the diggin' up of the grave personally. Of course, we all went along, wanting to get to the bottom of it.

"I don't know," Uncle Miles interrupted himself. "The rest of the story's grim. I don't know if you want to hear it."

I explained to him that I did.

"They dug down to the coffin and cleared the dirt off the top. And the first thing we all seen was that the nails on the lid was all wrenched loose. A gasp went up at that. And it was an easy matter to lift the lid."

Uncle Miles paused a minute and ran his old knobby hands over his eyes. "When they got the lid off, we all seen the problem. The dead man was a-layin' face down in his coffin with his arms throwed back behind him."

"You mean—"

"That's right. What with the swamp fever panic and all, they hadn't let the body cool. And they'd buried him alive. He must have come to hisself underground. And I reckon it drove him mad and he thrashed around before the air in the box give out."

"What happened then?" I whispered.

"Well, the damage was done, wasn't it? They turned him over. I won't tell you what he looked like in the face. He'd eaten off his mouth. Then they nailed the lid on good and shoveled back the earth. He rested easy then. Cleatus Watts took it severe. The ghost never come to him again. But Cleatus started goin' to revival meetings and church twice of a Sunday, and was just generally not very good company thereafter."

"I think I'd better be getting up to the house, Uncle Miles. It's late."

"Well, that's enough for one day, I reckon," Uncle Miles said. But I was already halfway to the back door by then.

After *The Ghost Belonged to Me* was published, teachers and librarians alerted me to the use of such stories-within-stories for short read-alouds to stir interest in reading the book. I followed up with another interior story in the sequel, *Ghosts I Have Been*. It involved a severed head in a bottle, but another sequence in that novel that I hadn't foreseen as a read-aloud, the ghost in the privy, turned out to be far more popular as a separate reading.

In dark moments during the writing of *The Ghost Belonged to Me,* I'd thought that creating a parallel Uncle Miles was more trouble than he was worth. But evidently not. An elderly character has appeared in each of my novels since, rising to the two books required to express the awe-inspiring Grandma Dowdel. Growing cannier, I haven't tried to lift them as directly from actual people. But now they're staples: Madame Malevich in *Are You in the House Alone?,* Grandmother Livingston in *Father Figure,* Miss Gertrude Dabney in *Ghosts I Have Been,* Lucius Pirie in *Unfinished Portrait of Jessica,* Polly Prior in *Remembering the Good Times,* Aunt Fay in *Strays Like Us,* and a reprobate old codger named Granddad Fuller in *Fair Weather.*

I need them. Young readers need them more. The old folks are there in the novels as counterbalances. They provide wisdom and seasoning won only through long lifetimes, and compassion unavailable from the peer group. They offer alternatives in the accelerating battle between parents and children, and glimpses of the problems and sorrows of old age for a young generation fixated on their own.

Some of the best writing for the young forges this link between the very old and the very young: Lawrence Yep's *Child of the Owl,* Mildred Taylor's *Roll of Thunder, Hear My Cry,* Katherine Paterson's *Jacob Have I Loved,* Cynthia Voigt's *Dicey's Song.*

Our books present foster grandparents for a generation robbed of extended families and elders: by divorce, suburban age segregation, Sun City, and the crime rate that keeps the old off the streets and out of sight. Moreover, this is a generation of the young who no longer have to write thank-you notes for gifts from grandparents, and so they rob themselves of their roots and are once again at the mercy of one another.

Besides, the battered old survivors who stalk through my pages embody the truth upon which all fiction turns: that in the long run, you will be held responsible for the consequences of your actions.

CHAPTER THREE

A novel is a community, and I come from one. It wasn't a suburb, and it wasn't inner city. It was a whole community with all the generations and the classes jumbled together, and with more subplots than any novel needs. All stories are family stories, and I came from one of those too.

That first world of mine was also the most nearly democratic universe I was ever to inhabit, though nobody wants a classless society, and Decatur, Illinois, wasn't. But there's nowhere to look now, not even there, to find that range of families all sending their children to the same schools in a system racially integrated well ahead of history.

The gilded children of the country-club crowd were there. So were the gaunt, ashen-faced children of the people who lived in tar paper, parked in the yard, and drank from the bottle on the front porch. We came to school from all sides of the track, and the school system, had we but known it, was a sociological powder keg. But it didn't blow sky-high until years after I'd left town.

A good many children who'd be lost now were saved then by the middle-class standards prevailing in the classrooms. Children whose lives were already disfigured by poverty, wealth, or some other affliction saw school as a clean, well-lighted place with teachers empowered by the system and the kind of droning routine the young demand. For some of us the standards of school were a clear echo of the values of home. For others school offered the only safe haven. Above its portals were invisibly carved the unspoken motto:

FORGET WHERE YOU CAME FROM,
ENTER HERE AND LEARN.

It started early, in ways small enough for a child to grasp. In first grade we were to turn up with the standard tin box of primary paint colors to learn how to mix them during art hour. Nancy S., who had a rich dentist for a daddy, arrived with a top-of-the-line palette of colors—thirty or forty hues—that wouldn't have embarrassed Vermeer. Miss Welch shook a regretful head at her.

"No, Nancy, take that paint box back to the store and get the regular kind." Thus in first grade we learned there were none too rich to have to mix their colors and find out all on their own that blue and yellow make green. The day was coming when challenging the buying power of the young was well beyond the teacher's jurisdiction.

We learned different things at different rates, of course. But somehow we were all literate by junior high without a remedial reading teacher in sight.

If school then had been what school became, a psychiatric social-welfare clinic with students as outpatients (the remedial, the gifted, the remedially gifted, the at-risk, the _____ challenged), I believe it would have impressed us less. School then was the great leveler, trying to treat every child as every other child's equal, an excellent corrective to what we children were trying to do to one another. It was only the gray dawn of the guidance-counselor era. Regarding a child as too messed-up to learn was considered poor form and self-fulfilling.

Besides, there was a community-wide embargo against airing your dirty laundry in public, and the schools reflected that. Schools neither lead nor follow; they reflect.

We had other ways of finding out what went on in the backgrounds of our schoolmates. This probing doubtless made a novelist out of me. But were the people who ran our schools right to sweep our personal problems under the rug?

Yes. We maintained the shreds of dignity important to a child, necessary for an adolescent. And the schools then could no more compensate for unfit parents, squalor, permissive rearing, and all the other grim truths in children's private lives than they can today. Schools clung to the function they could perform, teaching the two basics: literacy and delayed gratification.

Being a teacher was easier then, or I might not have planned to be one. There was no school drug traffic with its attendant problems: weapons, parents who refuse to know, the sudden wealth of seventh-graders, pushers better organized than the administration and untouchable. Truancy was light in a community where any teenager at large during the day was collected by the police and returned to the safety of school. No racial warfare raged down our halls because the principal wouldn't have permitted it.

Looming behind all this orderliness were the parents, family. Reputation counted, and some people had nothing else. One of their ways of making sure their children didn't let them down and show them up was to cooperate with the school. Another of the unofficial mottoes of the town had something to do with nipping things in the bud, and we knew whose buds they meant. Slung in this seamless safety net, we the young got away with whatever we could, and it was comfortingly little.

Teaching was a different deal then, in part because teachers were full citizens of the community. It wasn't an inner city they feared living in or a suburb they couldn't afford. You were liable to meet them anywhere. So were your parents. They had more energy than the teacher I became, because none of it was dissipated in trying to keep the peace. When teachers are more tired at the end of the day than the students, the wrong people are being educated.

Teaching is the art of calling people's bluffs, and our teachers had a hundred ways of doing that, some of them too subtle to see. A teacher I'd planned never to remember remains with me yet. His name was Mr. Merritt Pease, and he taught my least-favorite subject, seventh-grade industrial arts.

Under him we learned as much electrical repair as you could do without a license. He sent us home to replace all the frayed wiring on household appliances and to bring back lengths of frazzled cord and broken plugs for proof. This was a master stroke. At just that puberty time when we were trying hard to reject home and family, Mr. Pease was sending us back to rewire the house. While, by the way, the girls were taking home ec.

The lesson no teacher managed to convey was the big one, about change. The young believe that the future will be just like the present. Nobody could have convinced me that the world I was growing up in would vanish as thoroughly as my own father's barefoot Tom Sawyer country boyhood already had.

I only turned my back for a moment—college, the army, grad school—and when I looked around, all the healthy hypocrisies, the work ethic, the caring conspiracy of overlapping adults were already being stacked as cordwood for the bonfire coming in the later 1960's. Even in my first employment as a teacher, children as early as seventh grade came to school every morning secure in the knowledge that their parents and their teachers would never meet.

Why the people in my generation couldn't be the parents and the teachers we'd had, we never knew. Was it our permissive rearing method and television—Dr. Spock and Mr. Spock? Was it the divorce rate, the suburban move, the welfare state? Was it our need to buy our children's love and their upping of the ante? We never knew, and some of us still refuse to discuss it.

Years later, on the day I stopped teaching to write for my former students, I had to gather my thoughts. Teaching had been the art of compromise. As a writer for the same people, I again had to find that midpoint between me and them where we might be near enough to communicate without being struck dumb by our differences. Until that first evening of joblessness, I'd never fully grasped the term "generation gap." Though my students had cautioned me against reminiscing within their hearing, I couldn't let a novel live so near them that it didn't raise questions about their choices and offer options they didn't know they had.

I wasn't planning a lifelong career in writing that night—a body of work. I wondered if I could write one novel. But it was going to be a family story. And so has every novel after it. My teenage students were distanced from family life in ways I'd never known. But I sensed an empty victory here, suspecting they'd have traded their freedom for the security of belonging. Teenagers who hadn't been near a parent for days avidly watched a televised *Little House on the Prairie*. The most popular shows of that era were *M*A*S*H* and *Star Trek,* two stories of surrogate families.

In that field called "young-adult" books, we were to create a literature of family life for a generation who didn't have to be home on a school night, or had no home. It would be a literature of fathers for the fatherless, a literature to question girls who thought they had to demean their mothers in order to be women. A literature of the young looking everywhere for the stroking and structure of family.

My novels were to refer to traditional family while trying to reflect the altered worlds of young readers. As in teaching, here again I was hoping to offer a viewpoint the young weren't hearing. Though I was never going to write in my own voice, I was nonetheless there, lurking just beyond the margin of the page. In fact, the first line of fiction I ever wrote, the opening of *Don't Look and It Won't Hurt*—

> Out at the city limits, there's this sign that says: WELCOME TO CLAYPITTS, PEARL OF THE PRAIRIE, and if you'd believe that, you'd believe anything.

—sounds more like where I came from than where my readers were coming from.

And where were they coming from? I wondered that night.

Nearly half of them would be from single-parent and reconstituted families, some of them trailing whole tribes of stepparents. Some come from an almost familiar two-parent family, though barring the very rich and the very poor, more of them have two working parents. Some come from families where tragedy has struck, some from grandparents where they've been permanently parked by parents who've drifted away. Some of them, the children of my own friends, have parents working hard to provide good home lives for children who are rarely at home.

When letters from readers began to arrive, I was bewildered even more, and motivated, by all this variation in family life. From the students I'd just left I had some idea of what that variation cost them.

Don't Look and It Won't Hurt wasn't about my students. I was still too near them. It comes instead from the experiences of my friends Dr. and Mrs. Richard Hughes, who took in girls from a local home for unwed mothers in Evanston, Illinois. There I'd met girls waiting for their babies to be born. They were all different, and when I was getting ready to write, I asked the Hugheses what, beyond the obvious, they all had in common. They said the pattern hadn't varied. All the girls said they'd keep the baby, marry the father, and never return to their hometowns. In fact, they all gave up their babies, none married the father, and they all went home.

There was something of a bare outline in that. The rest of the story was up to me. After several drafts, I found I couldn't summon the sympathy to tell it from the viewpoint of the unwed mother. Supplied with a caseworker, hospital care, a surrogate family, she walks away from her own without a backward glance. She is, after all, the center of attention for the first time in her life.

The protagonist turned out to be one of her younger sisters who, not in the kind of trouble adults can no longer overlook, feels invisible and powerless. But her family has fragmented, and if anybody is going to hold them together, this fifteen-year-old must. In real life she might have believed that what had happened to her older sister was beyond her control. In a novel she goes after an older sister who's nowhere near mature enough to make any decision and hauls her back home.

From my first novel about an imperfect family I learned that the protagonist of a young-adult novel is not the case study or the victim. The protagonist is the young person who acts, not only for purposes of the story, but on behalf of the reader. It's action to give hope to young readers who feel helpless and to challenge the young who merely expect to be taken care of.

Don't Look and It Won't Hurt was published in 1972. In 1992 it was made into a movie called *Gas Food Lodging*. In the film's point-killing conclusion the younger sister is left in tears in a hospital corridor because the older sister refuses to come back home. She's planning to go to Dallas to be a model, which seemed to me a more ominous plan than the movie meant.

After that first novel, readers' letters and school visits took me in every direction. A visit to the schools of a western city where all but a couple of students in each class lived without fathers left me brooding over boys struggling through their teens without fathers there as touchstones.

That led to a novel called *Father Figure,* about a seventeen-year-old boy's attempts to compensate for a missing father, by playing the father-figure role for his own little brother, Byron. When they're almost forcibly reunited with their dad, Jim's whole careful construct of role-playing and denial is in jeopardy. They go to Florida to spend a summer with a stranger-dad:

> We pass a sign, COCONUT GROVE BUSINESS DISTRICT, and fol-
> low the arrow. Who is he? Lush? Lecher? Playboy? Pauper?
> All the above? The bonding on the Datsun's windshield is
> loose, breaking down the light into its component, rainbow
> parts. It hits Dad's legs. Tennis player? Swimmer? Over-the-
> hill jock? Who knows? Wait and see. Plenty of time. An
> entire summer in a place with no other season.

But of course there isn't plenty of time. They've lost too much already. The novel is about the time they have left, about whether they can use it to form some kind of tie beyond role-playing and macho posturing, or whether the threatened son will merely use this time to punish his father. The story is also about three characters who wonder if they can build an all-male family in a society without a pattern for that.

Nothing in my coming-of-age or family prepared me to write their story. Or did it? Confronting a generation of boys without fathers when I couldn't fathom growing up without my own may have been the novel's real inspiration. On the day I finished it, my father died, and at forty-three I was as lost as I would have been at any moment before.

Not every family is a minefield, not even now. In a time of intensifying sibling warfare, there can even still be younger sisters who idolize their older brothers and cherish their moments together to file away unforgotten. One of them is a girl named Verna Henderson in *Representing Super Doll*:

> But before Hal went back to Purdue, we had our little late-summer time together as usual. We never had to plan it. We'd always take off one early afternoon in the truck and head out to Persimmon Woods Reservoir.
>
> It's the water supply for the county, a man-made lake in the middle of nowhere. You have to open a gate to get to it, and we know where there's a rowboat. Out in the dead center of the reservoir it's like falling on a mirror—clouds above and clouds below. We always took books, but we never did any reading. We'd talk a little, drift a lot.
>
> I remember once when I was about eight and Hal was thirteen and we were out there. I don't know how it happened that he was rowing me around Persimmon that time.

Up till then he hadn't taken any more notice of me than was absolutely necessary. And it was almost evening that time, so we didn't have any business to be out there in the first place. But I'll never forget it.

The sun was just down to the treeline. There was every color there is in the sky. The lake seemed on fire, with that silhouette of shoreline black as cinders all around. And so quiet you had to whisper.

Hal began telling me a story. I think it was meant to spook me, and it did a little. But it went beyond that. He said that back in the days when they flooded the land to make the reservoir, there was a little town smack in the middle of it. One day the bulldozers just pushed their way in and all the people who lived there were told they had to get out.

This got me interested right away, so I asked him what the name of the town had been. He thought for a minute. Then he said it was Weavers Rest. (Now how do you suppose he came up with a name like that?)

Anyway, in the story all the people in the town had to scatter to the four winds. One day the water came in. A trickle down the gutters at first. Then rivers where the streets had been. Then only the second stories of the houses were left, with the curtains blowing out the windows. And things floating by, like sofa cushions and the children's toys.

Finally nothing cleared the waterline but the church steeple with the weather vane on top. And pretty soon it stuck up like a solitary cattail in the middle of the lake.

Then the water closed over that even. Hal made a little gur-
gling sound in his throat so I could hear exactly how the
water sounded when it swallowed up the weather vane.

He waited so I could absorb all this. Then he said the
boat we were in was just three feet above the church steeple.
That if we dropped a hook and line we'd snag the weather
vane sure as anything. I was gooseflesh and cockleburs all
over to think we were floating that very minute over a ghost
town, like ghosts ourselves. By then I'd clean forgotten that
I didn't believe the story anyway.

But Hal wasn't finished. He said that sometimes on a
very quiet evening, just around sundown, you could hear the
bells in the church steeple chiming. Of course you had to
listen with all your ears to hear bells tolling under water.
And if there was any other noise around, like fish jumping
or water lapping the boat, you wouldn't hear anything at all.

I remember my mouth was open but I wasn't making a
sound. It was quiet enough to hear the bells, quiet enough
to hear anything. And I thought about how the currents of
water really could drift through the belfry and ring the bells
in a soft, watery way. And how fish might be swimming in
and out where the stained-glass windows had been and
maybe an old crawdaddy on the pulpit.

It seemed so sad. And so beautiful. That little town,
Weavers Rest, where nobody lived, like the castle in an
aquarium. With the mossy bells gently ringing, making
hardly any noise, and no one to call to prayer anyway. And
there we were, Hal and I, hovering over it all while the lake

turned silvery around us. Of course I cried. Because it was so weird and lonesome and beautiful. Because Hal had told it.

Louise Fitzhugh named a novel *Nobody's Family Is Going to Change,* but they do. Family life keeps altering its shape and its course. There are more changes than the young want, because they like an even tenor to their days and adults around them playing the most stereotypical roles possible.

In *Princess Ashley* Chelsea is unnerved and threatened—and annoyed—that her family is moving across the country, and she'll have to start over in a new school. Bad enough if they were moving because of her father's job, but they're moving because of her mother's. "I didn't think it was right," says Chelsea with all the rigid sexism of sophomore year.

In churches and political arenas and in churches as political arenas, talk grows increasingly shrill about the traditional family now that nobody really can be sure what that means. The more uncertain people are, the shriller they become, the hungrier for scapegoats. More work for the novelist.

And now a newer phenomenon: college graduates returning home to their families because they aren't prepared to go anywhere else. Since they're returning home for reasons more emotional than economic, surely there's a novel in it.

CHAPTER FOUR

No, but really, *how did you get your start as a writer?* People persist, still hoping for a short answer.

Well, all right, I'm a writer because I was once a teacher. Though it's perfectly possible to write for the young without having taught, it wouldn't have been possible for me. After all, teaching is the craft of communicating with strangers in a language you can find, the craft of meeting absolute deadlines, the craft of trying to give *time* a shape.

These are the needs of the novelist.

It was as a teacher I learned to ask the writer's first question, that question that has to be answered before putting pen to paper:

Who are the people who might be willing to read what I might be able to write?

I found those people in my roll book. They were my students, the people I knew best and liked best. Their whims took precedence over my needs, and they had me outnumbered all day long. From our first hours together I knew things about them their parents dared never know. In their writing I read what they dared never say aloud within the hearing of their powerful peers. The voices in their pages still ring in mine.

I found my way to my first high-school students in 1961. Entering teaching in those days was the moral equivalent of moving to Rome just ahead of the Visigoths. The world in which we taught, the world we tried to prepare our students for, was running its last reel.

Moreover, we young teachers were the products of the education courses we'd had to take to be certified, those courses that hadn't prepared us for one minute of classroom survival. Our teacher training seemed to have little to do with the schooling we'd just been through. It was to relate even less to the teaching we were about to do. This was the sunrise of the "motivational" era, and we threw around such terms as "reading readiness," little knowing that few of our students would ever be ready to read unless they had to.

We were told that children must be motivated to learn, and if they aren't motivated, it's the teacher's fault. That was a lie, and a big one. It reckoned without the hard fact that the basis of all real learning is fear. Fear of the consequences of not learning, the fear of our own teachers' good opinions that had caused us to learn more than we'd meant to. It overlooked the realities that the nuts and bolts of learning are not creative play, that nobody can be tricked into learning. It blurred the root truth that reading is a discipline before it can be a pleasure.

In the education courses, we'd been told that the great impediment to learning is damaged self-esteem. My teaching was to reveal the reverse. My students' great learning disability that swept through the remedial and the gifted alike was the fixed idea that what they didn't already know wasn't worth knowing. It was a conviction that dealt a mortal blow to geography, history, foreign language, and was to ride Latin teachers out of most schools on a rail.

What we were never told was that in each year of their learning from preschool to grad school, the young look for a source of absolute authority before they can look for themselves. The young demand leaders they cannot reason with. Children arrive for their first days of school disoriented by the power struggles they've already won over their parents, though the education courses were mum on the subject. Nobody told us that young people who cannot find a source of unyielding authority among adults will look elsewhere.

There was no end to what I hadn't learned in those education courses. My first high-school students, who weren't a lot younger than I was, seemed to be inhabiting another planet, and were. They were suburban. Vast school complexes were rising from former farmland like something out of science fiction. People in the millions were voting with their feet and marching out of cities to the subdivisions fanning out from these new education facilities. I'd come from a real town and dreamed of cities. Now I'd washed up in Middle Earth. Given the size of the parking lot, I mistook the school on the first day for a shopping mall, which wasn't far wrong.

The teaching jobs were out here, with salary schedules more attractive than the treeless terrain. I blundered onto this alien soil without a guideline. It would be another fifteen years before Judith Guest wrote *Ordinary People,* and longer than that before M. E. Kerr's *Night Kites.* I had to learn on my own that a lot of people move to suburbs not to deal with life's problems, but to avoid them, that there are people who believe they deserve utopia because they paid so much for the house. I learned on the job that there are families who don't believe bad things happen to good people, that they will punish the bearer of bad news.

If the town had a motto, it must have been ALL THAT WE DO, WE DO FOR OUR CHILDREN, triggering an unintended response in those children, a troublesome mix of arrogance and guilt. Families had moved here specifically for the quality education promised, and so the ball was clearly in the teachers' court. It was up to us to justify their faith, even to maintain the value of their real estate. The school responded by declaring every student college material, a short-term anesthetic, with another unintended effect: The students recognized school as a place where teachers could fail, but they couldn't.

Viewed in retrospect, it was still a comparatively innocent world. Though they were already in the process of shifting full responsibility for their children onto the school, there were more parents attending P.T.A. meetings than would dare show their faces now. The prom was still held in the school gym and not in a downtown Chicago hotel as combination dance and sleepover. The divorce rate wasn't yet astronomical. But the breadwinners' long suburban commute, the decline of the dinner table, the glaring fact that adolescents were rarely at home, left us teachers as the adults our students knew best. It conjured up a fearful image: all those tract-house family rooms with nobody in them. And from us teachers, the students wanted parenting we couldn't provide. They wanted acceptance for what they were, not teaching to change them.

But it was the hermetic provinciality that got to me first. In one of my classroom defeats, I was extolling the cultural advantages of Chicago, some fifteen miles down the expressway, and I was being met by stone walls in a class of eleventh-graders.

"But what are you going to tell people," I said, "when you get out in the world?" (Fatal phrase.) "You'll have to tell them you're from Chicago, but you don't know anything about the place."

A boy at the back said almost patiently, "We'll tell them we're from Glenburnie." (Let's say.)

"But they'll never have heard of it," I said.

Sighs rose from behind the stone walls. Now I'd annoyed them. A girl in the front row skewered me with a look. "Everybody in the world knows Glenburnie," she said in the level tone she used on parents.

I never sold them on the glories of the city where their incomes were earned, and Carl Sandburg wasn't the help I'd hoped. But it didn't stop me. I went off in search of the literature, the lesson plan, the sound bite—anything to let in a little of the outside world. There were, after all, a few in the room secretly dreaming of escape, of bright-lights-big-city, but the peer-approved view was of the city as a crime-ridden environment for people who were their social and intellectual inferiors. Hearing from me that Saul Bellow was an inner-city dweller wasn't much of an epiphany for them either.

I'd never seen this much conformity before, this strictly enforced by children and this heavily subsidized by parents. But they weren't as uniform as they looked. By labeling every child college material, the school was built on a fault line. Most of the victims were invisible. One of them lay comatose across his desk in my tenth-grade English class. He came alive, I'd heard, only in the industrial arts department, a repository for lost souls. His name was Scott, and I was sorely tempted to let him lie dormant because he wasn't giving trouble.

He wasn't interested, and he wasn't preparing, and I didn't seem to have a motivation for him. Then one afternoon I was threading my way through the parking lot past the MGs back to where the faculty parked. My old Studebaker Lark wouldn't turn over.

Scott appeared at my wing window. The parking lot was his domain. He rapped on the window, saying, "This yours? Jeez, a Studebaker. I might have figured. Raise your hood." He was under it awhile. "Gimme the keys," he said finally.

Scott gave the Studebaker the only expert tune-up it ever had. It made it through the year and so did Scott. I tried to pay him for his labor, but he said, "What for? I don't pay you to teach me."

"I don't teach you anything," I said. But from then on he let me teach him, a little. No education course had prepared me for Scott, but maybe he was an education course.

I don't know that I've lifted more than bits of him for any of my novels. But in young-adult books, we were to create a lot of young characters going doggedly about the work of being themselves and looking for themselves, surrounded by contemporaries all in uniform, looking for group identity and leaders, and waiting to be taken care of. Our protagonists were going to act not only on behalf of the readers, but in defiance of the government of their peers.

No, wait, I've just come across Scott in a book I was to write twenty years later, *Close Enough to Touch*. He's called Matt now:

I was a tenth-grader, your basic kid. Nobody in particular. Still feeling fairly out of it because I hadn't come to town till junior high and even by then most of the groups were already pretty sewed up.

I was just topping out at six feet tall and trying not to fall down when I ran. Remembering to use Ban roll-on deodorant every day and shaving every other. Thinking about boosting myself up to the bottom rung of the honor roll to help lower the insurance premiums once I got my license.

And getting Dad to pop for the '65 El Camino crying out for racing stripes and new vinyl at the back of the "previously owned" Chevy lot. Picking through parts places for four matching hubcap covers and chrome stripping just in case. Getting a part-time job when I turned sixteen to clinch the deal.

And thinking about girls in an abstract way, checking through their postage-stamp pictures in the yearbook. Contrasting these with the full-color of my fantasies.

The parking lot plays its own role in *Close Enough to Touch*. After all, the scope of the parking lot lapping all four sides of a school was my lasting first impression of suburbia, more ground that the young stake out remote from the possibility of adult interference.

In the novel Matt has suffered an unthinkable loss. He has lost the first girl he ever loved. Still, he has to go back to school on the day after her funeral, more alone than he's ever been. And he has to get through the parking lot first.

I park in a plowed field three blocks away. The school squats on the horizon. Walking back, I kill time by matching cars with drivers. Everybody's here already, and still I'm not late. Time has slowed down recently, and it's impossible not to be early.

I have no trouble identifying the silver Porche 924 Turbo, parked at an angle with its incredible snout blocking half a parking space reserved for faculty. It belongs to Royce Eburt, stud senior. In half an hour a P.A. announcement will flood the school, requesting him to move it, which should be good for a laugh in the locker room. The day is already predictable, prepackaged.

Bill Matlack's tooling around the crowded concrete in front of the main doors astride his Honda 450, herding the pedestrians. Right and left hands rest over throttle and clutch. He's moving slow, and his boot's already drifting back to the kickstand.

Creeping opposite, also parade-slow, Sheri Martinson is

piloting her midnight-blue Celica Supra with Royce Eburt riding shotgun. The king and queen of the seniors are conducting their morning motorcade.

If anybody remembers yesterday, they seem to have themselves pretty well under control. I cross the parade route where Alice Kirby's standing, waiting for Bill Matlack to part with his Honda.

She sees me, and her face drops into a sad mask. "Oh, Matt, listen, I'm really wrecked about—"

But Bill's swerved the Honda up beside us. It slips sideways under his crotch, and he throws out a steadying boot. "Smokin' and strokin'," he says loud in my ear, looking past me at Alice. He guns the Honda in neutral, blatting out all human sound. Alice lifts her shoulders and we're all off the hook. The bell seems to have rung during the Honda sound. I go with the flow.

By the time I began a writing career, most of the young were suburbanites. Most mail from readers bore suburban postmarks and still does. Most of the invitations to visit schools and libraries come from there. A lot of us writers were going to set our novels in suburbia, and not only for undeniably recognizable settings.

Two of my novels, *Are You in the House Alone?* and *Remembering the Good Times,* are on issues so widespread, they might have been set anywhere. They were to be classified as single-problem novels, but no novel dares be that. Growing up is a whole skein of problems. In *Are You in the House Alone?* a high-school girl is targeted, stalked, and sexually attacked by a classmate. Even in the 1970's, when it was written, rape was our fastest-growing, least-reported crime, and its chief victims were teenage girls.

Problem enough, but I thought the suburbs made it worse. In the novel Gail is a suburban girl, without street smarts. No one has told her that a rapist is rarely a stranger, and it's beyond her to believe that anybody in her peer group would hurt her. If she can imagine an enemy at all, it would have her mother's face. Her family has moved to the suburbs for the kind of cosmetic safety that works better for parents than for their children.

> After a few years and a lot of colonial restoration, a lot of Dutch doors and old glass in new frames and split-shake shingles and carriage lamps beside the doors. And everything in Williamsburg red or Williamsburg green or Williamsburg beige—we tended to look flinty-eyed on new arrivals too.

The young will live in the smallest worlds possible. Gail's lulls her with promises it can't keep, where she actually opens the door while she's baby-sitting. The community empowers her rapist too. In a specifically suburban way he's already been forgiven everything, and his family has the kind of local prominence that assures him that he's above the law.

In *Are You in the House Alone?* I took on the suburbs, and television too. I didn't write the novel to tell the young what rape is. They already knew that. I wrote it to point out that in real life the guilty aren't apprehended just before the final commercial. In real life, in our implementation of the laws, it's the victim who serves a kind of sentence, and when the crime is rape, the sentence is for life.

This was for many years my most widely read book, but none of the readers who write back notice any criticism in the portrayal of the suburban setting. They're merely outraged that justice doesn't prevail. May they be outraged enough to change our legal system when their day comes.

I wrote *Are You in the House Alone?* to indicate that life is not a television show. It was made into one. Just before the final commercial, the rapist (played by a very young Dennis Quaid) is apprehended and separated from society, on cue.

When *Remembering the Good Times* was published, a novel about a promising teenage boy who kills himself might have been set in any location. By 1985 suicide was one of the three major killers of young people. Research led me to the high concentrations of adolescent suicide in Plano, Texas; Westchester County, New York; and Beverly Hills, California.

A boy driven by his internal need for future success is drawn nearer the edge by a slack suburban school moving at a pace slow enough to maintain the self-esteem of the least motivated. Trav sends out a major message about his frustration in an interchange with his teacher Ms. Slater:

"But you're a very good student," Sherrie Slater said. "You're excellent, Trav."

"How would you know?" He was almost bending over her now. "How would you know? I'm coasting. We're all coasting. This is recess."

She looked away from him, out across the empty rows. The halls outside were full and loud, but we were trapped in this vacuum. I was wishing people would come in and this would stop. "There are people in the class," she said, "who don't have your abilities, Trav, and they—"

"Then they need work too," he said, getting louder. He jammed his hands down on her desk, grinding the heels of them into the metal top. "We're losing time. I know the rest of them don't care, but they're losing. We're not getting any better. We're not getting anywhere."

A suburban parent might find that scene surreal, at best misplaced. Wouldn't a boy be far more frustrated by the pace of some drugged and demoralized, poverty-stricken inner-city school? All the more reason to set it in the suburbs, where the statistics of this tragedy had led me.

I wasn't to set all of my novels in the suburbs where most of them are read. Novels have that other opportunity to demonstrate that life is actually going on elsewhere. *Father Figure* is about a summer in the life of a New York City private-school boy. *Representing Super Doll* is a gentle (or as gentle as I can manage) comedy about an honest farm girl bused into the high school of the nearest small city. *Bel-Air Bambi and the Mall Rats* is about a family of show-business kids uprooted from Bel-Air, California—not quite a suburb in the usual definition—who find themselves going to school in the ultrarustic country village where their dad grew up. In *Voices After Midnight* the modern-day members of a suburban California family make it all the way to the New York of 1888. In both *Ghosts I Have Been* and

Amanda/Miranda readers are even invited to sink on the *Titanic*. In *Lost in Cyberspace* and *The Great Interactive Dream Machine* the time travel is digital and computer-driven.

Novels need to raise questions no one else is raising in the lives of readers, and not every novel need be doom-laden. *Secrets of the Shopping Mall* is meant to raise its questions about the consumerism and peer grouping of the young out there beyond the city limits by means of knockabout satire.

Well before we were forced to notice South-Central in Los Angeles and the cores of every other big city being run by underclass youth gangs that were the only family their members had, it was happening among the affluent children of aspiring families. It was in the suburbs where the young became a separate society, as we young faculty fogies noticed. It wasn't shaping up as a subculture either; it was becoming the dominant culture of the nation, the way most young people lived.

Suburbs became the historic, off-center crossroads where postwar affluence, permissive rearing, and the breakup of older family patterns met. There at these crossroads rose schools to educate the whole child, where children turned to one another for the only rules they could find with teeth in them.

Somewhere in the 1960's the tide turned, and power shifted from adults to children. I saw it passing across the desk in a suburban classroom. A literature was on the way to ask the young the questions they no longer heard from parents and teachers.

Those first adolescent students of mine left their mark. Long after we parted company, after they'd joined me in the adult world, I was to write something called:

A Teenager's Prayer

Oh, Supreme Being, and I don't mean me:
Give me the vision to see my parents as human beings
because if they aren't, what does that make me?
Give me vocabulary because the more I say you know,
the less anyone does.
Give me freedom from television because I'm beginning
to distrust its happy endings.
Give me sex education to correct what I first heard
from thirteen-year-olds.
Give me homework to keep me from flunking Free Time.
Give me a map of the world so I may see that this town
and I are not the center of it.
Give me the knowledge that conformity is the enemy of
friendship.
Give me the understanding that nobody grows up in a group,
so that I may find my own way.
Give me limits so I will know I'm loved.
And give me nothing I haven't earned so that this adolescence
will not last forever.

Amen

CHAPTER FIVE

The great American theme in the final third of the twentieth century was the tribalizing of the young. The separate society they formed was better understood by the music, film, and clothing industries than by the schools. The young appointed contemporaries as leaders and fell in behind them. Adolescence became less a preparation for adulthood and more a holding pattern, a celebration of gains already consolidated. Graduate school became a growth industry for people resisting an adulthood that they saw as a loss of power.

I'd thought of all this as a result of the suburban distances between parent and teacher, parent and child, workplace and home, the suburb as setting where the young never saw themselves as less than a majority. But life called my bluff. It was a call I'd been waiting for all my life, the offer of a teaching job in New York.

It was the laboratory school of a college on the Upper East Side of Manhattan, with the world at our feet and reaching for the sky. Though I thought I'd seen history being made in the suburbs, I hadn't seen anything yet. Just as I turned up, this cutting-edge urban school was about to detonate with the two issues that defined the late 1960's: ethnic/racial school integration and Vietnam War protests.

I went, wondering what I had to offer teenagers already in the city I'd taken thirty years to achieve. I wondered what they'd be like.

They were quicker even than the suburbanites to judge adults: educationally, politically, morally—lightning quick. But their rules for us were not to apply to them, and they were as determined as the young anywhere not to be held responsible for the consequences of their actions.

My first impression of this new place was the old issue of grades. Who got what grade was clearly a more pressing issue to the students here than world peace and universal brotherhood. It was a school for the academically gifted.

Our old habit of overpraising those we couldn't control was catching up with us everywhere now. Nothing in my background offered much by way of preparation for this either. I dated from a time when college professors and even some high-school teachers looked out over us on the first day of the term and said, "I give two A's in this class. I wonder who you are."

But we'd long since begun raising grades and lowering

expectations to make winners out of everybody. Chester E. Finn, Jr., writes:

> We are very good in this country about building up children's self-esteem in education. If only it had some relationship to the truth.[1]

It starts early. Chester Finn's book cites a student-teacher who avoided introducing her second-graders to words they didn't know so that "the children should feel good about themselves."

The resulting grade-inflation had seemed to work for everybody, making schools look good, students feel good, tranquilizing parents. Now the whole nefarious business of refusing to scar students with accurate grades was coming home to roost on the new English teacher in a school for the academically gifted.

Assigning grades to compositions was an old irritation. Putting language to work doesn't respond well to a grade scale. Of course, a good many papers were failures. They were mindless rough drafts. They were all one long misshapen paragraph. They'd been written during commercial breaks. They were nowhere near the assigned topic or any other.

Weirdly, the English department's policy in this school was to give numerical grades on all student work. In going over a batch of papers in a tenth-grade class, I gave one a 96. I don't know what a 96 on a composition means, but in this case I'd tempered justice with mercy. It was a good paper with room for

---

1. *We Must Take Charge: Our Schools and Our Future,* The Free Press, 1991.

improvement because there always is. I gave the paper a 96 along with a careful commentary that was to go unread, and thought we might all live with that.

On the day I returned the papers, the author of that one was soon at my desk, tapping a boot. "What's the meaning of this grade?" she asked.

"It means that I'd like to see another draft," I said. "It's far too good not to be better."

"You're new," she said. "I guess you don't know what we're up against. We're heading for the best colleges in the country."

The implication that I hadn't gone to one was clear. "Do you think a ninety-six on a sophomore-year paper will kill your chances?" I said.

"It might," she said, "if you make a habit of it. I don't know what my parents are going to think of this."

"Send them to see me," I said, which is the way to quench almost any controversy with a tenth-grader.

The flaw in the inflated grade is that it can never be good enough. That girl didn't really believe a grade as low as 96 on a paper would keep her out of Brown University. (It didn't.) She wasn't worried about her parents either. She feared no adult. She was conducting the usual personal competition with her peer group in which grades were one weapon among many. In a different kind of school, cheerleading might have been a pivotal issue.

We wish students learned for the love of it, but that's asking too much of people that young who have already been promised too much. The inflated grade leads to more than the inflated ego. It sets people up for failure. A little lifetime later, in the 1988 International Achievement Test, the thirteen-year-olds of the U.S. team finished last in mathematics. But when they were asked to estimate their standing, they ranked themselves first.

Places are always different once you get there. New York was a smaller town than I expected, though it lacked a small town's social contract. The local notion that civilization ceased at the Lincoln Tunnel made the suburbs seem, too late, Parisian in their worldliness. The faculty was heavy-laden with teachers who had graduated from the school, something I'd associated with a remote country town.

Students couldn't be asked for absence excuses because they might have been attending a war protest rally somewhere. The debate team folded because there couldn't be two views on the war, or anything else. Bullhorned demonstrations were orchestrated against South Africa, though the students had segregated the school from within.

On the blackboard I wrote, from Eric Hoffer:

IT IS EASIER TO LOVE HUMANITY AS A WHOLE

THAN TO LOVE ONE'S NEIGHBOR

But it turned no tides. The distance between word and deed yawned at our feet. The creed of political correctness was being born, possibly in that very school, and here I was again, uncomprehending, at a flash point in history.

It was the late 1960's, a time to be remembered, forgotten, rewritten. Political activism was another weapon in the hands of the young in their quest for strong leaders. Once I said wickedly to a urologist's daughter in a Marxist work shirt, "That organizer of your spontaneous demonstrations is old enough to be your father."

A girl dropped like a stone out of her seat into the aisle in one of my afternoon classes. This and not Woodstock was my introduction to the drug culture. We rushed her to the hospital, and when we contacted her mother, she thought the girl lived with her grandmother. When we contacted the grandmother, she thought the girl lived with her mother.

The F I'd given as a final grade for a student who'd never been in my class was neatly changed on her official record by an unseen hand—to a B. I wasn't settling in, but the days wobbled on.

Then something happened that changed every moment of the rest of my life. Though I'm still dead set against the idea of the autobiographical novel, it was an occurrence that was to inform every one of my books, the idea in all of them that we learn chiefly from the experience we would have avoided if we could. It happened to me. I was assigned to the junior-high division of the school.

Nobody chooses to teach junior high. You get assigned. I had to start over from scratch. My files burgeoned with the unworkable: all those *King Lear* lesson plans; the Cavalier poets, mimeographed; those heady advanced placement comp assignments; that unit on Aristophanes that had almost worked.

I looked around one day in the midst of life, and I was the only one in the room not going through puberty. I was also the only one in the room who wasn't gifted, but then, I was used to that. And perhaps this is the time to mention that this was a girls' school.

I hadn't had the education course I needed, the one called "Communicating with the Pubescent," because it doesn't exist. Puberty is the darkest time of life, for while it is the death of childhood, it isn't the birth of reason. You wake up one terrible morning, and nothing works, and everything's the wrong size. I have a private theory that puberty lowers the IQ ten points, just as car ownership at sixteen lowers it another five.

The seventh-graders were the first in this junior high/senior high. I'd never seen people this young this close. And talk about a mixed bag. Those from Roman Catholic parochial schools knew some grammar. Those from the open classrooms of progressive schools hadn't yet learned how to sit down. Those fresh from the public schools of the New York City system were looking everywhere except at me to see who was in charge. The only trait they had in common with their older sisters in the upper school was the desire for A's for themselves and B's for their friends. I hadn't yet burned out on teaching, but I was beginning to smolder. On the other hand, this looked like a whole new line of work.

Where, for example, was the reading curriculum for these people? The junior-high reading list has been a thorny problem for the teacher in better days than those, and continues to be for the teacher who hasn't discovered young-adult books. You can get just so much mileage out of *The Red Pony*.

On the day I entered the junior-high universe, the English faculty were banning a book. It was one I'd been counting on. But they were expunging it with maximum efficiency and without publicity by pulling it off the reading list and disposing of the class sets. It was Harper Lee's *To Kill a Mockingbird.* The reason given was that it "celebrated white, bourgeois values," the values of the people banning it, as far as I could see.[1]

I did the only thing I could think of. I entered my classroom, wrote title and author across the blackboard, and told the eighth-graders the simple truth—that the book on the board had been removed for their well-being.

So that was one book they read, but what else? Just across the Hudson River, a New Jersey housewife was writing *Are You There, God? It's Me, Margaret.,* but she wasn't writing fast enough to save me. My students were either too young or too old for most of the prose and poetry I could scout out.

"Irrelevant" was their favorite judgment, and they were quick to apply it to my best-meant readings. I began to study them and their responses, to second-guess them as I had never done before. They were hard to figure. Puberty may be the final unexplained phenomenon, the black hole wherein all inquiry flounders. I went looking for just one novel they couldn't call irrelevant.

Happily, there was a great one, *The Member of the Wedding* by Carson McCullers. Surely the protagonist, Frankie Adams, is still the most telling portrayal of a girl at that age. The novel catches her like a fly in amber and holds her through a static

---

1. A quarter of a century later the October 1, 1992, issue of *USA Today* (p. 6D) reported that a high-school Black Student Union in Atherton, California, "objected to a school production of *To Kill a Mockingbird* because it provided only 'subservient' roles for black students. School officials canceled the play." As the century turned, *Catcher in the Rye* was being assailed in certain university quarters for being "insufficiently multicultural."

summer. With too much gusto I ordered a class set and handed out the copies one fatal Friday.

On the following Monday they'd all been returned to a pile on my desk. A spokeswoman for the class said, briefly, "We won't be reading a book about a crazy girl."

I had to give that some thought. (For one thing, they were reading *I Never Promised You a Rose Garden* by Hannah Green all on their own.) Frankie Adams is beset by problems: the angst of being too young and too old all in the same endless summer. Her body and her emotions betray her at every turn, and everybody on earth has a party to go to but her. She isn't crazy, though. Insanity would have been an escape.

I read the novel again, trying to see it through the eyes of a thirteen-year-old girl. It took me five nights; I kept slipping into myself, my own admiration for the book. It wasn't written for the young, of course. It was for readers who'd made a safe passage to adulthood and dared to look back.

My students had called Frankie crazy because they couldn't distance themselves far enough from her, and she was no one they wanted to be. If they'd read to the end, they'd have found no solace there either. The novel leaves Frankie suspended still, no nearer an evolution than before. This captures wonderfully the mood of puberty, the mood of the class. And they weren't having it. My attempt to sell Frankie Adams to a room full of Frankie Adamses gave me ideas I wouldn't have had in trying to prepare high-school students for college.

Here was what teaching is: the attempt to get people to make that connection between themselves and the page. *The Member of the Wedding* was the novel that made a novelist out of me. I could never be Carson McCullers, whom my students rejected. I couldn't be Judy Blume either, whom they were about to embrace. But in the desperation for readings that any junior-high English teacher knows, I began to wonder if I could write something for the earliest teenager readers that would be true enough to suit me, hopeful enough to suit them.

At the time, however, I was more concerned about getting them to write than in motivating myself. Though it wouldn't have surprised an experienced junior-high teacher, I was mightily struck by my students' naked hostility. Very little of it was directed at me. They came in the door bickering and went out quibbling. I'd thought puberty sulked, but this bunch was more aggressive than that.

The only writing they did with passion was on the notes they tirelessly circulated. Thinking to harness some of this energy, I hit upon a writing assignment that I was altogether too pleased with. One day when they came bristling in, I told them to take out paper, and I dictated the opening line of an in-class composition. It was:

"The one thing that really makes me mad is . . ."

I invited them to fill the page, and they fell to it. That was the first day of complete classroom quiet, and my hopes were high until the end of the day. At home that night I never quite got beyond the first line of the top paper:

"The one thing that really makes me mad is when my mother talks back to me."

That wasn't the first of my writing ideas that closed out of town. At least it cured me of asking them to keep journals. The flaw in the assignment was that it was writing-as-therapy. Reaching for the undeniably relevant, I'd helped them open a can of worms that was already open. When it came to expressing their emotions, they'd been doing that all along in the circulated notes. We have a bad American habit of encouraging students to do what they're already doing.

I had to go looking for other writing assignments. You have to reach farther for the pubescent, and the real stumbling block to composition was this group's belief that among the gifted, class discussions were enough.

I wouldn't have chosen to teach junior high, no indeed. But you know something? I liked them. Sooner or later they'd tell you anything. Their defenses were a mile high, but paper-thin. They used language I hadn't heard since the army. They were evil enough to one another to inspire a book I was to write called *Dreamland Lake*. But I liked them, and there were spaced moments of wonderful, antic innocence.

One spring day a seventh-grader came up with a magazine open to an illustrated article for me to read. It was about Old Order Amish farm families in Lancaster, Pennsylvania. The next day I handed it back to her, vaguely bemused, saying I though it was interesting.

"We thought you'd like it," she said.

"Why?"

"Well, you're not Jewish, are you?"

"No, I'm not."

"And you're not Catholic," she said, "because on that day in March you didn't have ashes on your forehead."

"No, I'm not Catholic."

"Well, then," she said, smiling up and shrugging. "What's left?"

The idea that being Amish is the only option that remained to me hit my brain like a thunderbolt. I stood there adrift in the intense provinciality of both New York and other people's puberty, hung up between laughter and tears, where I often was.

After a year of total immersion in junior high, I was to teach back and forth between there and senior high. This, too, was new and revealing. High-schoolers looked different now: bigger, more heavily defended, farther from adults as they grew nearer adulthood. Students who'd been good writers in eighth grade weren't as good in tenth, not having had to write anything much in the time between. And every semester there were fewer students in the classroom and more bullhorns in the streets below.

This era was so full of sudden bad news that we adults staggered between denial and rephrasing. A suspicious number of people could not remember having voted for Johnson, while in the faculty lounge we people of the word looked for a new pseudoclinical vocabulary to define what we could no longer control.

I went home one afternoon, overheated by the decline and fall of practically everything in sight. I wrote a poem, though I wasn't given to that sort of thing. The title was a girl's name chosen at random. "Nancy":

Trying hard to look hard,
You balance with one ankle turning under,
Your eyes, sloping off your face,
Wanting only the chosen word overheard.

I wonder at your clothes:
The expensive skirt,
The leather boots,
Clinging to your calves,
Plinths for thighs from sculpture.

Hearing the little moan
Behind your voice,
The little tug that signals:
"I am communicating with the enemy."

I wait with prideful patience,
For I have heard you after every class—
What is it? Twenty times this term?
And each time my patience seems more marvelous to me.

Speaking of relevance, explaining where I went wrong.
Showing me the existential skull beneath my skin-deep philosophy,
Wanting me only to know that I have failed you,
Have driven you to the barricades.

My mind wanders among your threats of anarchy,
Blood in the streets. The tenacity of you!

Every day sullen; every day burning
With borrowed fire.

Are we making love, you and I,
Across this fumed-oak desk?
You who would bridge the generation gap
With human chains of the immolated underprivileged.

In the faculty meeting, someone rose, saying,
Ladies and gentlemen, we are confronted with
The first generation that was picked up
Every time it cried.

And from this tyranny of solicitude
I sent you back, beloved,
To the barricades
In your expensive skirt.

I sent it to *Saturday Review,* the only magazine I read regularly in those days of nocturnal paper-grading.

Reader, they published it.

That poem is, at best, a period piece of those times, a thumbnail sketch of the generation who are the parents now. But in its publication I caught a whiff of the distant scent of printer's ink. Words from my typewriter were on sale at the magazine store.[1] A copy of *Saturday Review* went silently from hand to hand in the faculty lounge.

1. June 21, 1969.

I quit my teaching job one spring in the early 1970's, seven years before Lois Duncan wrote *Killing Mr. Griffin*. I hung up my tenure and went home after seventh period to try to write a novel.

I left teaching, but not lightly, because I knew I wasn't coming back. In the faculty lounge they were holding out for better times. They were saying that we were going through a bad patch, that one day the racial and ethnic integration of the school would work and the students would meld seamlessly in a rainbow coalition that we adults could learn from. But I didn't believe the young could achieve that without a framework so strong that they were forbidden to hurt one another.

In the faculty room they were saying that when the Vietnam War was finally lost, our students would have won a great victory over the authority we represented and would be magnanimous victors. They would give up following strangers and would return to the classroom to begin learning again. But I didn't believe that either.

In teaching I'd found the people I wanted to write for, two groups of them, in fact. The adolescents of high school and the pubescent of junior high, and I wanted to begin with the younger ones because they seemed to be in the greatest need. They were at the age when we've always lost most people to reading. They were the people I knew best, and yet I'd never known as much about them as I needed to. That would help me write too. It kept me on their trail. We're more impelled to write for what we don't know about people than what we do. A novel is a question, not an answer.

I'd failed as a teacher. I'd never convinced enough students that they didn't know what they thought until they'd written it down, that books provide alternatives, that fiction can be truer than fact.

But teaching made a writer out of me. It gave me a priceless viewpoint for a writer: to pay more attention to what people do than to what they say. In the classroom, I'd discovered that you can teach people or you can sentimentalize them, but you can't do both. If you see them only as victims, of society or the self, you stop teaching and start treating. You can't write about them either. Victims aren't to be held accountable, but protagonists have to be. A novel isn't a remedial program that excuses you from learning because of your disadvantaged background or test scores. A novel isn't an elective course you can drop when it threatens to challenge you. Novels aren't gifted programs that promise you happy endings you don't have to earn.

The premise of all storytelling is that in the long run you will be held responsible for the consequences of your actions.

In the classroom, I'd noticed that nobody grows up in a group. People grow up, if at all, one at a time in spite of the group. That opened a new door, because a novel is the celebration of the individual. The underlying theme of all my novels was to be that you will never begin to grow up until you declare your independence from your peers.

Teaching offered me the tools. I had to keep them sharp and find some more, but they gave me a start. Though I resigned from teaching in order to write, teaching is a job you never really quit. You just go on and on, trying to turn life into lesson plans. Years after my tenure and pension plan were but fond memories, I wrote something called:

A Teacher's Prayer

Oh God, I'm only a teacher,
  And it's lonely work because I'm the only member of my
  species in the room.
  I like kids, and I love my subject matter,
  And I have higher hopes for these kids of mine than they
  have for themselves:
    I want them to create. They want to consume.
    I want them to love the world. They want the world to love
    them.
    I want every day to be different. They want every day to be
    the same.
    I want them to burn with zeal, about something. They
    want to be cool, about everything.
    I want them to think. They want me to tell them.
    I want the bell to ring. They want the bell to ring.
Oh God, I'm a teacher,
  I'm not their buddy. I don't want to be. I've seen
  what they do to their buddies.
  I'm not their parent, and yet they're looking high
  and low for parents and can't seem to find them.
  I'm their teacher. I don't want them to take me at
  my word. I want them to find the words.
Oh God, I'm a teacher,
  So I'm perfectly willing to move mountains if You'll
  send me some hands for my end of the lever:
    Send me a couple of administrators who care more
    about standards than they care about their jobs.

Send me the occasional parent who sees in me a colleague,
not a scapegoat.
Send me a few kids every semester willing to brave
their peers in order to learn.
Oh God, I'm only a teacher,
I want to make bricks. Could you send me some straw?

Amen

And How Do You Get Your Ideas?

From observation, not experience; from research, not autobiography. If Ernest Hemingway really had fought all those wars and bulls, if he really had climbed all those mountains and caught all those fish, if he really had loved all those women, he wouldn't have had the time to write, let alone the need. We get our ideas from memories, usually of other people, even other people's memories. And from other people's books. We're always looking to other people for our stories, then creating other people to tell them.

For me, writing a novel is like making a quilt. You gather bright scraps from other people's lives, and then you stitch them together in a pattern of your own. I've never made a quilt, but I like the analogy.

CHAPTER SIX

Through the memorable years that I taught, coming of age changed its shape, even its direction. With new freedom to be themselves, the young wanted to be one another.

The seventh-grade title character of Phyllis Reynolds Naylor's *All but Alice* says:

> "If we were all standing in a line that stretched around the entire state of Maryland, I don't want anyone to be able to tell me from anyone else."

They believed even more than we had in group identity as a mask for personal uncertainty. That need had made a generation of them easy prey to the political and narcotic massing of the collectivist late 1960's. It also provided new opportunities for novelists to raise inconvenient questions in the most entertaining ways we could think of.

Life sharpened the themes for novels as celebrations of the individual: to explore that gap between word and deed; to move beyond blame-shifting; to search for the self in a landscape without the old landmarks; to see the book as a source of alternatives, the protagonist as role model.

I doubt if thoughts this cosmic were at home in my head during the writing of that first novel. I wrote it one word at a time, feeling my way down many a dead end, just as I've written all the rest: pausing for an agonizing reappraisal at the foot of every page, spotting for the unnecessary word, the prewilted image, writing six drafts. Marveling at how much harder it is to write a novel than to teach one, how much easier to criticize than create.

Luckily, I wasn't alone in the room. Frankie Adams from *The Member of the Wedding* hung there in the corner. She'd been that real, responsible portrayal of a girl, whom my students had rejected, but I couldn't. There's evidence in the first novel, *Don't Look and It Won't Hurt,* that Frankie was giving me the only advice I had, and warnings.

Whether in first person or third, a novel is told by its characters. My protagonists would have to be something more than recognizable. They'd need to be a blend of the real and the ideal. They'd have to be able to do something the readers couldn't, or wouldn't. They could be acted upon only early in the story; then they'd have to act. It would have helped to have Chris Crutcher's *Running Loose* there on the desk, but he hadn't written it yet.

In my first novel Carol Patterson has to empower herself. She has to run away, leaving herself behind, to bring home an erring sister. Though she's just the age to draw away from her family, Carol has to draw hers together.

Frankie was guiding my hand in another direction. Carol in *Don't Look and It Won't Hurt* is fifteen and three-quarters, for a younger readership in junior high. One of Frankie's classroom drawbacks had been that she was the same age as the readers.

Young people don't want to read about characters their age. They want to read about people who are two years older. At whatever age they are, they believe that real life doesn't start until twenty-four months later, when they will be fully evolved. They don't want to be adults. They want something better than that: They want to be in high school.

Junior high wants to read about senior high. High-school freshmen want to read about anybody with a driver's license. The gap narrows then, and eleventh-graders are fixated on seniors. They're cool to reading about *now*. Nothing's happening *now*.

What I learned for the first book I forgot in the second. *Dreamland Lake* was written for seventh-graders about seventh-graders. They're boys—Flip, Brian, Elvan—perhaps because I was still too near the rigors of a girls' school. And anyway, seventh grade is its own sex.

They're boys enacting the friendships I'd seen in all my junior-high classes. At puberty there are no equal partnerships. The friendships were composed of one follower, one leader, and a common enemy to give them a cause.

But there's movement in *Dreamland Lake,* because this is a

novel and not real life. Flip isn't an imaginative leader, and Brian's beginning to think for himself. In real life the relationship would stumble on at least through puberty. In an ideal world Brian would tell Flip that he was tired of being ordered around and a little bored. He'd cut his losses and walk away. In the novel the two of them remain locked in their role-playing a moment too long, and they destroy Elvan, the common enemy whom they have in large part created.

> "Come on, let's go after him."
> "Let's go the other way."
> "No, we'll just tail him till he hears us behind him. It'll keep him moving. Come on."
> We jumped the creek together and kicked along the path, half running, making extra noise. But I think Elvan was too far ahead to hear. We loped along, bent over under the low branches, and came out into the open by the end of the lake.
> . . . I was looking straight up along the path, past the barricades at the approach to the bridge. Flip stopped dead. He threw out an arm and opened his mouth. Then I saw Elvan. He'd gone over the Park Department sawhorses that warn you off the bridge. And he was pounding over it. Almost at the top of the arch over the middle of the lake.
> Flip cupped his hands over his mouth and yelled, "Elvan, stop!"

But it's too late. In the first rational moment of his life, Flip tries to call off the games. But Elvan is lost in an accidental death, and Flip and Brian are responsible. This is the costly conclusion to their friendship, and their childhood. Brian walks away a moment too late, haunted for life. Flip will rewrite the episode as pure accident, because leaders can forgive themselves anything.

If you don't have a happy ending for the young, you have to do some fast talking. The novel is a morality play with a dash of inspiration drawn from *A Separate Peace*. It issues a challenge few seventh-graders are ready for, but until it began to be a classroom reading, almost all the letters about the book came from fifth-graders. They're hooked by the melodrama of the first page:

> There was a dead man in the weeds up at the woodsy end of Dreamland Lake.

They're drawn by the friendship of Flip and Brian. Fifth-graders think anything that happens in seventh grade is great and that friendship is the greatest.

In the midst of the book the boys build a murder-mystery fantasy around an old tramp's body they've found in the woods. I'd hoped readers would see through that, would grasp that the boys are fantasizing to keep a failing friendship going. But few readers did, fewer still of the fifth-graders. I'd hoped nobody would misread the book as a mystery story. I hoped in vain. It won a prize from the Mystery Writers of America.

By then I must have known that writers write one thing, readers read another.

For the third novel I tried to get a grip on myself. To learn that all-important skill, pacing, I wrote a page-turner. Writing that bogs down is an eternal problem. Writing about characters bogged down in puberty is fatal. In *Through a Brief Darkness*

Karen is in sixth grade on the first page. By page eighteen, she's sixteen. Would that actual puberty moved at that clip, and better yet, Karen spends part of it on horseback.

The tone is light too, or meant to be. After the somber message of *Dreamland Lake* I wanted to try for something more conventionally action-packed, with a touch of the Gothic novel. Having won a mystery prize for a novel that wasn't one, I wanted to write a mystery (which won no prize).

It's the story of a girl distanced from her father because he's a Mafia figure. She's abducted by his enemies. In real life, kidnap victims hope to be rescued. At best they hope to escape. But books are better than real life, and characters must do what readers can't. Karen must not only escape, but round on her abductors and nail them.

I worked to make this a brisk, entertaining, roller-coaster read. My readers thought otherwise. In the letters that still come, they're drawn to the serious kernel of the story, the relationship between father and daughter and their failure to communicate. Readers looked beyond the artifice of plot and pace to the human connection and linked it to their own. It was, after all, the story of the lonely daughter of a remote father.

Had I been trying to write down to them? I hope not, but if I had, they turned me around. We can get caught up in the surface tastes of the young for science fiction, romance, horse stories, sports sagas, fantasy, and the grotesque. We do better to realize that they read, as all fiction readers do, for the human relationships they have, or want.

It wasn't until the fifth book that a girl named Blossom Culp entered my life. Only I would make the connection between

Frankie Adams and Blossom Culp. With only age in common, Blossom is otherwise everything Frankie isn't.

Blossom began as a supporting character in *The Ghost Belonged to Me,* that story about Alexander Armsworth and his uncle Miles. There's a dead girl in that story, the ghost of Inez Dumaine, but I found I needed a live one.

Blossom crept up on my blind side in a way entirely characteristic of her when I cast her as Alexander's foil. I'd created her by turning him inside out. He's a boy, she's a girl. He's rich, she's poor. He's spruce, she's bedraggled. More to the point, he's a conformist, and she's an original.

She's Frankie's opposite too. Being thirteen is the least of Blossom's worries. She has disadvantages Frankie never thought of. I've heaped them on her. She's unpopular, unattractive, shapeless, hungry. And while every thirteen-year-old girl thinks her mother is a witch, Blossom's mama *is* a witch.

But Blossom returns fire. Her indomitable spirit and outrageous spunk are meant to reverberate all the way back to fifth-grade readers as an alternative to the sulks and self-pity of puberty. And the cloning, especially that.

There was a Blossom Culp in every class I ever taught, the class outcast, the designated pariah. Like Blossom, they were sometimes set apart by poverty—and that towering issue: clothing choice. But there were also other factors, mostly invisible to the adult eye, that kept the rejects out of the loop, out of the running in the peer-group games. In the classroom I'd felt powerless to save them or in some way make it up to them. Blossom was something I could do.

Even as a secondary character she began to develop along the lines of a life force. With nothing to lose, nothing to fall back on, she's far more adventuresome and resourceful than Alexander, the carefully hand-reared boy with the thirteen-year-old male's fragile dignity to protect.

As a second-banana character, Blossom wasn't the best idea I ever had. She was too strong for the part, too sassy and verbal and inventive. I kept having to rein her in. She not only met trouble halfway, she created it. And when the truth proved inadequate, she told whoppers. She invented her life. Then, when the book was published and filmed, she received more reader mail than Alexander.

It appeared that young readers identify most strongly with precisely the characters they wouldn't want to sit next to at school. Blossom isn't the first underdog in print, but she came along when the peer group had uninhibited power to turn in fury on nonconformists, and she was met with a warm response from both camps. The reception led to three more novels about her and Alexander, told emphatically in her voice. These four novels are the first I'd set in the past, 1913 and 1914, but the hierarchy of a small town is meant to reflect patterns far more modern.

From *Ghosts I Have Been:*

There are girls in this town who pass their time up on their porches doing fancywork on embroidery hoops. You can also see them going about in surreys or on the back seats of autos with their mothers, paying calls in white gloves. They're all as alike as gingerbread figures in skirts. My name is Blossom Culp, and I've always lived by my wits.

In Blossom there's more than a hint of Huckleberry Finn, that naively wise, single-parented ragamuffin clinging to the raw edges of Hannibal. Mark Twain can't be matched, but he can inspire. Blossom's Hannibal is the Bluff City of my own uncle Miles's memories of Decatur, Illinois, a microcosm of all the pomposities of the world. Novels forever question the class system, and the young want a more rigid class structure than adults could endure.

Alexander is from new money yearning for social respectability. He's at home in the third largest house in town, though it suffers from an old tragedy in the turret and a ghost in the barn loft. After the first book he becomes Blossom's foil in a relationship that never bursts into romance, to the consternation of many readers, none of them male.

Blossom's disadvantages would cause gridlock in a modern welfare system. Some of the richest scenes throughout the books are between her and her stymied teachers, confronted by this upstart child, both needy and overwhelming.

Bluff City isn't even her hometown. She's an interloper onto this stylized scene because she and her mother have already been run out of Sikeston, Missouri, by "a more progressive element." Blossom launches herself every morning with half a cup of coffee inside her to face the world, fortified by knowing that "there is more to be learned about a town from the wrong side of the tracks than the right."

To do honor to iconoclasts, you have to portray the conformists. Blossom goes off every day to a school dominated by a peer-group leader named Letty Shambaugh, whose father owns

the Select Drygoods Company. There was also a Letty Shambaugh in every class I ever taught, every one I visit. The fact that
she is sweet on Alexander Armsworth doesn't improve Blossom's
opinion of her.

> From *Blossom Culp and the Sleep of Death:*
>
> I'll say one thing and one thing only for Letty Sham-
> baugh. Small though her mind is, she keeps it busy. Letty
> finds it hard to work education into her full schedule, as
> she's president of both the freshman class and a private club
> of girls called the Sunny Thoughts and Busy Fingers
> Sisterhood. This particular gang wastes no time in holding
> elections because Letty is president for life . . .
>
> The Sunny Thoughts and Busy Fingers Sisterhood girls
> have been looking down on me ever since fourth grade,
> when I hit town, and I'll have to live longer than our teacher
> Miss Blankenship even to darken their door.

How true. Blossom will never be a joiner as long as I live. But
she turns up as an unwelcome guest in the lives of the mis-
named Sunny Thoughts and Busy Fingers girls often enough to
give Letty the grief she has coming to her.

Apart from an almost terminal temerity, Blossom has one
compensatory advantage. She has a touch of the supersensory in
her makeup and possibly her ancestry. She can do a little light
time travel and claims to have "the Second Sight."

These talents ally her with Alexander, who can see ghosts,
though he fears and denies a trait the other boys don't have.
The supernatural element is there by reader request. It broad-

ens the readership to include boys and girls and, as I learned early, alerts Walt Disney Productions.

The supernatural gloss is only a device, and I think of the novels as period comedies of manners to parallel the present. Through her misfiring time travel Blossom draws even nearer her readers in *The Dreadful Future of Blossom Culp*. She plummets through time to meet a modern-day boy who believes he must have conjured her up on his computer. Blossom, as visitor from the past, has just materialized at Jeremy's house in Bluffleigh Heights and has encountered his bellicose older sister.

"That is one bad-tempered girl," I remarked. "What's put her in such a mean mood?"

"Tiffany?" Jeremy said. "Oh, that's as good as she gets. Basically, I guess it's because we're from a broken home."

I scanned the room again. It looked all right to me. "The roof fell in on me and Mama once," I said. "And the porch has fallen off the house a couple of times."

Jeremy stared. "Not that kind of broken home," he explained. "I mean our mom and dad don't live together anymore. Dad's living in a singles condo complex out on the Airport Highway."

"Oh, well, shoot," I responded. "I'm in a similar situation myself. The last time we saw my paw, he was hopping a freight to Centralia."

Jeremy poked his spectacles higher on his nose. "You mean in olden times you people had divorce?"

"Well, I don't know about divorce," I said. "That sounds expensive."

Blossom's readers seem to value her most for her extrasensory powers. I value her most for her valiant independence. We meet, though, in the core of her character. There's another element in her, buried beneath the bravado and the extravagant claims to have the Second Sight. She's young and easily hurt, and she has her pride. She'd love to be loved. Of all my heroes and heroines, she may be the most vulnerable.

Blossom Culp has become by far my most popular character. She receives mail that I do not.

After those four books Blossom appears again, under another name in a very different kind of novel. In *Remembering the Good Times* a modern boy named Buck likes a girl named Kate. One evening he appears at her back door, to find it guarded by an old lady in a wheelchair.

Her finger came up then, bent in about six places, and she sighted along it at me. "I'm the third oldest woman in Slocum Township. But when it comes to meanness, I'm Number One." Her finger pointed to the porch roof. "I'm too mean to die."

The lightning bugs were out, dull sparks in the night. Then there was a shape at the back door.

"Polly," someone said through the screen, "are you talking to yourself again?"

"Might as well be," the old lady said, and Kate stepped out onto the porch.

She was the same Kate, but the dark softened her chopped-off hair and made her look taller and even thinner.

She walked over and ran her hand along the back of the wheelchair.

"You got yourself a caller, Katie," the old lady said. "I bet a nickel he's sweet on you. Looky there, he brought you a mess of tomatoes." She sat back in the chair to feel Kate's arm behind her and to watch me squirm.

"Ah . . . no. It was Irene, she said—"

"Hi, Buck," Kate said.

"I knew you knew him." The old lady nodded. "Boys is going to be thicker around here than speck eyes on a potato. I'll have to clean my shotgun."

"This is Polly Prior," Kate said to me. "She's my great-grandmother, Buck."

"Oh boy, am I old," said Polly Prior. "I was lucky they didn't wing me when they shot McKinley."

"My mother and I live with her. It's Polly's house and her orchard."

"So watch your step," said Polly Prior.

Of all the elderly characters in my novels, Polly Prior is the best I can do, and she is Blossom Culp grown old.

CHAPTER SEVEN

As postrevolutionary role models, the main characters of books for the young have new jobs to perform. They're even linguistic role models. They can speak the length of a book without ever saying "like" or "you know." Our characters speak as our readers would if they had the immediate and radical speech correction they need. Our protagonists have a lot to do well beyond the range of the cardboard Hardy Boys. They have to be more resourceful than Nancy Drew, swifter than Tom.

But Huckleberry Finn never dies, and our books feature Hucks of both sexes, and they're often suburban. Most of them are more plausible portrayals than Blossom's. We can't give them all Second Sight. Sharing traits with the readers, they have to be imperfect enough for improvement and willing to stand up for who they are. They have to take one step nearer maturity in an age when maturing itself has become an elective, and they must show readers the way, give them the word. "It's me gets to tell the truth," says Jerome Foxworthy in Bruce Brooks's *The Moves Make the Man*.

Not every novel is told against the backdrop of the peer group, though we need every one that is. We need no novels about how to fit in. Popularity and acceptance cost too much now. Some of our characters have to create their own worlds because they were born somehow or other outside the peer-group pale: Blossom, Dennis Covington's Lizard, Jerome in *The Moves Make the Man*. And perhaps most memorable of all, Shawn McDaniel in Terry Trueman's *Stuck in Neutral*.

More of our stories enact the conversion from conformity. The characters begin as does the football player in Chris Crutcher's *Running Loose*. It takes him till senior year to realize he's being packaged like meat to promote the career of a corrupt and racist coach. In real life he'd likely hold his breath until he graduated. In a novel he rises up, says no, and takes his lumps.

In Will Hobbs's *Downriver,* Jessie finds her peer group when she's sent off to a fresh-air camp for teens already in trouble with the law. "Hoods in the Woods," they call themselves.

> You'd think no one had ever rolled a car before. It was an accident, one that could have happened to anyone. And not just a kid, either. The police had blown it all out of proportion. We weren't drunk. And we were way out in the country, where there shouldn't have been any other cars.

Her blame-shifting is reasoned enough to take in both herself and the readers. She and her fellow Hoods run away from the camp to shoot the Grand Canyon rapids of the Colorado River without a permit, a map, or an adult to guide them. The trip becomes adolescence itself, a group tour to prove that the rules don't apply to you.

Their peer leader is a manipulative charismatic who knows just how to eliminate the remnants of real family from his followers: "In a lot of countries you're grown up when you're thirteen. Your father's trying to psych you out so he can stay in control!"

Long after Jessie sees through Troy, she's still resisting the truth, the independent step she needs to take away from him. But this is a novel, and so at last she rids herself of dominance she'd have called abuse had it come from a parent.

In *Downriver* the peer leader is Troy. In Robert Cormier's *The Chocolate War* he's Archie Costello, and in Cormier's *We All Fall Down* he's Harry Flowers. In Scott Johnson's *One of the Boys* he's Marty. In Rosa Guy's *The Music of Summer* she's Cathy. In *Princess Ashley* she's Ashley Packard.

As title character, Ashley is the antagonist, not the protagonist. She's the girl I notice at once in every school I visit, the girl who never walks alone. She makes her entrances with her entourage, ladies-in-waiting dressed as she echoes. Her body language is significant. She sits aside, turned away from the front of the room, from any other focus. She conducts business through every class, against a distant rumble of unobtrusive adult voices.

I don't get letters from her. She's not liable to be a reader. She hardly has the time, and so I wonder. What would it be like to go to school because it was your power base, not a preparation? How would it feel to be burdened with that much authority that early in life? How much does she fear a future where she might not hold this sway? The novel raises these questions, if not the great imponderable: For her own sake and others, why have adults let her happen?

Her portrait in the novel extends to include her male counterpart, Craig, two golden youths whose command is so naturally rooted that nobody remembers when it began.

The narrator of *Princess Ashley* is Chelsea, one of Ashley's willing followers who throws away most of high school belonging instead of becoming. As new girl in town she believes the heavens have opened when she's accepted into Ashley's magic circle, never wondering why. She delays her conversion as long as she can—two years. Before Chelsea has exhausted herself by finding excuses for her ruler, readers have the opportunity to see through Ashley's tireless manipulation, if they will.

Princess Ashley isn't my first approach to the alternative hierarchy the young set up to replace adult power failure. Here, though, the issue takes center stage because the drug of choice in adolescence is conformity.

In writing this book I looked for the maximum of realism that fiction allows. Fiction is based on the realities of relationships, and our sets are dressed with familiar trappings. But in *Princess Ashley* I wanted more. This is the most extensively documented of my books. I have thick files of research on the issues in earlier novels, on rape, on suicide, a hefty folder on shopping malls.

For this one I gathered material on what is arguably the most status-ridden high school in America, the one I know where the students were most thoroughly in charge. I had friends on the faculty, friends who sent their children there. I went myself as visiting author. I wanted nothing in the novel that wasn't directly based on what was in fact happening among the students in that school, their patterns and parties, their home lives and school lives, the vast open stretches of their free time. By this fourteenth novel I could walk down a school hall close enough to eavesdrop and take notes that were legible later. Every creative-writing course should mandate shorthand.

It was the most engrossing research I'd ever done. I kept digging until I had brief, euphoric, eerie moments of being on the other side and thought I really did know what it's like to be there, in young shoes.

A girl patiently explained to me the process of having the birth date on her I.D. altered so she could buy liquor. Momentarily I could imagine driving the car Daddy bought me down to the little man at the back of the shop on Dempster Avenue to have him professionally falsify the numbers. It was but one errand among many, run to subvert a law no adult had a right or any conceivable reason to impose.

A girl died in that suburb while I was doing research. Coming home drunk again from a party, she drove her van into a tree. Her schoolmates made a kind of shrine along the curb, leaving flowers and pictures, mementoes. In death she was far more popular than ever she'd been in life. For a more lasting memorial her classmates planned a fund-raising party, and held it off school grounds so they could serve liquor.

I learned a lot, and I paid for it. Surely I'd already known that real life is too overwritten for fiction. The outlooks and actions of real young people didn't cast them well in their own parts. And for a novel I needed hope, but found only certainty.

The characters in the novel—Chelsea, Ashley, Craig—pale in comparison. A character I needed for contrast and commentary in this completely self-referential society was one I had to create far more on my own. He's a supporting character named Pod Johnson.

> He planted his hands on where his hips should be and looked around. His eyes glazed over. They're deep blue—set a little too close together. But very blue. He happened to be looking at a line of six girls, probably juniors, all carrying fake Gucci bags, which were still very big that year.
>
> "Say, listen," he said, "where are we? Who are all these people? I haven't seen this many people since the last tractor pull. And how come they all look alike? Help, I'm being held prisoner in a clone factory."

I conjured up Pod in defiance of my research, to play a secondary, counterpoint role. In another novel he'd be only the love interest for Chelsea, and in fact she'd be safer in the backseat of his car than she is being programmed around the clock by an unstable group leader. "Did you happen to know you're a lot better person away from the bunch?" Pod asks her. "You're more fun. You're more . . . real."

And Chelsea replies in anger, "No, I hadn't noticed. It doesn't happen to be true. You just want to turn around and take me home?"

Pod offers the alternative in the novel, though it takes more time for Chelsea to discover she has an option. Still, she wakes up sooner than most followers. The novel concludes at the end of junior year, giving her another high-school year to start the search for herself and real friends. Pod was an individualist all along. In the country of conformists, the kid growing up at his own pace on his own terms is heroic whether I've cast him in the lead role or not. In Pod, I'd come up with another Blossom Culp, and sure enough, he's getting some reader mail I hadn't foreseen.

I wrote *Princess Ashley* as a high-school story for junior-high readers. But the young don't like warnings, and a novel has to be something more than that. When Chelsea gets to go to all the right parties, the readers get to go along. There's a lot of surface glamour, and the cover of the book plays its part. It depicts the powder-blue Mustang convertible delivered on cue at Ashley's sixteenth birthday party. But I hoped young readers would see through Ashley and the world she creates for her followers. I hoped the readers would cheer Chelsea on to a direction of her own.

According to the letters, not every reader is ready for this, and I inadvertently gave them a way out. When Ashley loses her band of followers, she has no more reason to attend that school and merely instructs her father to send her to boarding school.

Craig is a peer leader without this survival instinct. Unlike Ashley, he's desperately looking for limits. As Pod steadily grows up in the background of the novel, Craig as steadily follows a downward spiral. At the end he self-destructs. He doesn't die; it's worse than that.

Craig is drunk through most of the story, and a good many

readers focus on the book as an antialcohol message, skimming neatly over conformity as the real addiction described. Craig blurs the central issue for these readers. The great dream of adolescence is to replace your family with the surrogate family circle of your peers. There are readers who thoroughly identify with Chelsea when she believes her mother is never right and her leader is never wrong, but who aren't ready to comprehend her conversion. It was in the classroom I learned that you don't win them all.

Now I've moved on to other books, still looking for the divide between source and story, the shortest distance between character and reader. I have to keep relearning that central truth about writing—that fiction must provide something that real life withholds.

We never write about ordinary people. Oh, there are unconvertible conformists and people running to type at the edges of our stories as a sort of Greek chorus, and all the peer-group leaders are hauntingly alike. But we celebrate rebels and rebels-to-be, Huck Finns looking for themselves and the way out of town. Young people who are beginning to run for their lives.

Those of us who were teachers don't believe much in phases. It's parents who can explain away their children's behavior as phases they're going through. Teachers are less sure. Teachers have evidence that people don't grow up till they have to. There are people still going through puberty in senior year. A system of school that issues diplomas to people who can't read them retards their development further, and they look elsewhere for status and identity.

There are people well along in adult life who still believe that being in the right place with the right people will mask their personal inadequacies. Long after graduation there are people voting in a bloc, counting on club membership, trying to live in the smallest worlds possible. In adult life there are still people searching for scapegoats and finding them. They spur us on, too, to create young characters who won't become them.

But where do those characters come from? They can't be too real, or ideal. They have to be freshly original and yet remind readers of somebody they know.

"A life collects itself within my own life—" Sue Ellen Bridgers says. "A separate identity I am always questioning. What do you think? How do you feel? What did you do next."[1]

Characters are assembled from parts: observations, notes, memories, other people's books. We put words in their mouths and then sit back warily, hoping they'll speak for themselves and tell us who they are.

"They accrete," Nadine Gordimer says. "They are composites. Who knows where they come from? You hear a phrase, you notice a look, all sorts of impressions come to you."[2]

And on dark nights at the desk, you pray they'll keep coming.

1. From *Reading Their World,* Boynton/Cook Publishers, 1992.

2. *The New York Times,* January 1, 1991.

CHAPTER EIGHT

And we get our ideas not only from other people's books but from our own as well. Way loads on to way in writing, and the elements in one book echo later. The readers' response to one book calls forth the next.

Judith Guest's *Ordinary People* inspired me to write *Father Figure*. *Ordinary People* is a novel written for adults about the guilt of survivors. It's a theme to transcend time and geography, but no setting could have worked better than Lake Forest, Illinois, a perfect, privileged place that isn't zoned for tragedy.

It's the story of a family who aren't there for one another in the aftermath of a terrible loss. A son dies in a boating accident and in dying kills the life of the family. The story turns upon the adolescent younger brother, Conrad, but his parents, too, are isolated by their grief. Only at the end do Conrad and his father, as the sole survivors of the family, begin to turn to each other for the rudiments of solace. They resort to each other only because of the mother's unwillingness and inability to bear the emotional burden for them.

I couldn't have written a sequel to this novel that doesn't need one. But it gave me a kind of permission to write *Father Figure* and then more novels about fathers and sons and the emotional frigidity of American males, their use of women to do their emoting, their fear of their own tears and vulnerability.

Father Figure is that story of the long-absent father abruptly reunited with his two sons, told by the angry, threatened older son, Jim. It's about three desperate males: child, adolescent, and adult, who respond to an enforced intimacy by looking for a woman who can nurture them all and act as a buffer between them.

They find her in Marietta, who is as attractive to all three of them as I can make her. But she's chilled by the cold distances between them and refuses to be used. When she disengages in a graceful, final way, they're left with one another and what they might be able to build in the way of emotional bridges. Finally Jim has to make an unthinkable sacrifice to rid himself of his hostile defenses and take that first step into adulthood. Before he does, father and son achieve the fumbling beginnings of cautious contact.

> Dad puts his arms out. I put my arms out. We grapple a little. Then step together for a moment, Byron leaning against us both. We bang each other on the back, make it hearty, make it quick. Then we make the break.

A sadly small gain, perhaps, as a conclusion, but a beginning. Like all novels for the young, *Father Figure* ends not with happily-ever-after, but with a new beginning, as *Ordinary People* does.

The fates of those two books were entwined in an unexpected way. *Father Figure* was the first to be made into a movie. David Susskind produced it from a script that highlighted the father's role as a star vehicle for the actor Hal Linden. Still, the film ends with the same scene that concludes the novel, which was a consolation. More encouraging still, Jim's role was played brilliantly by the young Timothy Hutton. In his next role, he won an Academy Award as Conrad Jarrett in *Ordinary People*.

Father Figure led to *Close Enough to Touch,* in the unrealized hope that Timothy Hutton would play Matt Moran. The book was written as a response to the Harlequin-style romances in which emotions are women's work and men merely stand and deliver. Life imitates art, especially bad art.

The first paperback cover for *Close Enough to Touch* suggests a standard romance, but it's told by a boy and it begins as romances end. At the foot of the first page Matt is at last able to say, "I love you, Dory. I always will."

And Dory replies, "I love you too, Matt. What took you so long?"

But we never see her again. She dies suddenly, and Matt thinks what any seventeen-year-old boy would think, that he's lost his only chance for love, forever. Yet he's not her widower. The only role assigned him is as pallbearer, one of six. He has to go to school on the day after her burial. But first he has to get through the night between.

Matt has a father who would lay down his life to spare his

son's pain. But he lacks an emotional vocabulary. He goes to bed early that night, leaving his wife, Beth, Matt's young stepmother, to cope.

> She's washed all the makeup off her face, improving herself. She borders on beautiful and doesn't even know it. I've never tried anything as bold as telling her. I don't even give her a Valentine. They probably don't make them for stepmothers.
>
> "You know," she says in a careful voice, "I never really knew Dory. . . . Shall I not say anything more?"
>
> "No. Talk. Nobody's talked to me all day. All I've heard are words."
>
> She thinks about that and doesn't seem to find it crazy talk. "I did like her," she says. "I mean I don't know if we'd have had anything in common. She was like the girls I sort of knew when I was in high school. The ones in the college-prep classes. I was in secretarial and business English, but they were always, you know—"
>
> "The stars," I say.
>
> She searches my face. "Well, yes. They all seemed to have plans, and all I had were dreams."

In the watches of the night around a kitchen table, an uncertain stepmother, too young to be the mother of this grieving boy, does what she can. But in this novel women can't be his whole answer, though Beth isn't the last one he turns to.

He's a boy who's been romancing above his station in the taut social system of a suburban high school. Dory had come from the elevated Glenburnie Woods part of town. Matt lives in an apartment complex along a feeder road. His family are working people who appear to want no more than they have. He doesn't enjoy a higher standard of living than his own parents, and he seems to be the only kid in town with a grandmother.

Dory had been his only tie with the society of school. Then out of a sense of their own superior solidarity, a girl named Linda from Dory's group draws Matt back into their circle. It's only an abortive interlude, though it might have been the solution in real life, or in a romance novel.

But I won't allow it. No one but Matt can solve his problems. His loss is the hard opportunity to find his own emotional reserves. The burden of the story rests on his solitude and his attempts to cure himself with the false medicine of drinking and running away. In fact, I thought of calling this novel, ironically, *Simple Solutions,* but the editor said it would sound like a chemistry textbook.

In time Matt meets a very different girl, coming out of left field. Margaret exists more because I want her to than in the name of reality. Moreover, she's an interesting older woman—a senior. She's also in business for herself in the midst of the herd instinct that rules her schoolmates. Like all my heroines, she's independent, forthright, outspoken, and goal-oriented. My heroines never faint.

Margaret can deal with a young stepbrother who would drive a real-life teenage girl wild and out of the house. She's even come to guarded terms with a stepmother who's a psychologist. Margaret is more highly evolved than her peer group, much nearer adulthood. She and Matt meet in best romantic-novel tradition, by chance, away from the routine of school.

She can't solve Matt's problems for him either, though she can help. Her idea of being an enabler, though, shocks some readers. Instead of sympathizing with him over his loss, she reminds him that she isn't much interested in Dory, or in anyone that conventional.

The very word *conventional* baffles Matt, as it does many readers. Matt's healing process develops out of its necessary solitary stage, nudged by Margaret's unsentimental challenges.

Do the two of them marry and live happily ever after? Some readers are mildly irate or merely confused by the lack of the white wedding they believe should wrap up every novel ever written. But it would be immoral to give the young everything they want. The story ends at a new beginning. What will happen after the final page is to be written in the minds of the readers. Novels aren't television shows.

A novel with some of the characteristics of a romance explores a boy's particular problems in coming to terms with sorrow, in letting himself cry. The book was to give boys an emotional voice. Now I get letters from girls who want to meet the boy.

But a more worrisome response to this novel came when I was going around the country to talk about it in classrooms. To spark students' interest I read the first two scenes of the book, Matt's declaration of love to Dory and a wounded, doomed doe they see along the side of a busy highway. I asked the students if they could imagine what was coming next. Only a few suspected that the girl might die, that the doomed animal fore-shadowed that. They were shocked to hear it.

We moved on to discussions of Matt's response to his loss, the point of the book. What might a boy in his situation do? Then it was my turn to be shocked. In every classroom a boy said Matt could solve his problem and banish his grief by killing himself. Suicide, much on their minds, seemed to be a solution. I anguished over that. I tried to rephrase the question. Still, a boy would mention suicide.

In a junior high school where the seventh-graders had already lost three of the boys in their class to suicide, I bottomed out, with questions for myself. What would it have been like for me to lose three classmates in seventh grade? Would suicide have been a viable alternative?

This unwelcome reaction to *Close Enough to Touch* led to *Remembering the Good Times*. In my youth the great killer of the young was polio. As children we knew other children who had died—been tortured to death—by this disease. By 1985 the three great killers of the young, ages fifteen to twenty-four, were suicide, drunk driving, and murder. And there is no Salk vaccine for these.

We lose a young person to suicide every ninety minutes, that we know of. I had a lot of painful learning to do to put me in this picture: research in the California and New York statewide suicide-prevention programs, and among suicide-hotline volunteers. The California State Highway Patrol spoke of two kinds of fatal car wrecks involving boys: those with skid marks and those without. During the year that I began gathering information, seven teenagers in Plano, Texas, killed themselves. Five boys in New York's Westchester and Putnam counties died by their own hands, all in the same month.

Suicide is the ultimate lonely act; yet some die as a peer group. They fall under the influence of a magnetic leader, often an older teen, who gives them the discipline and parenting they've been looking for. Then he leads them to death. Newspaper accounts still come to me about groups of the young, dead in some suburban garage, because people send you your strongest research after the book is written.

In newspaper files I looked at the yearbook faces of the dead, and most of them had died alone. When I learned that three times as many girls threaten suicide and three times as many boys commit suicide, I knew early that the novel would be about a boy.

Professor George Hendry of the Princeton Theological Seminary cited the "easy life and empty optimism" of a generation left unchallenged. His research led him, and me, to the suburbs as the profile of the victim emerged. He was a boy identified as academically gifted, living in apparently easy circumstances, and driven in an environment that presses the young to succeed without imposing the necessary skills and disciplines for success.

But he couldn't be a personality printout or a list of clinical symptoms, and a novel has to be something more than a warning. I chose to tell it as the story of a friendship, an even more appealing format for young readers than romance. In a book, they're looking for companionship, for better friends than they have. It's the idealized story of a friendship, unlikely because it's formed in junior high between two boys and a girl across the gender barrier. It gathers strength in high school as a haven against the lonely crowds of adolescence. The three young people, Buck, Trav, and Kate, reach out for a fourth member, Kate's ancient great-grandmother, Polly Prior.

Their friendship will be shattered by Trav's suicide. Nobody kills himself out of a clear blue sky. Trav was sending out messages all along, even before the novel begins. Without an emotional vocabulary to express the chaos inside him, he expresses it in political and economic terms. And nobody understands. His young friends admire him too much to see the trouble he's in. And Polly, clinging to life on any terms, can't imagine anyone that young throwing away a life before it has begun.

Even in Trav's penultimate act of giving away his possessions, his friends are uneasy but uncomprehending still, like the readers. To Kate, Trav gives his stuffed Paddington Bear from childhood. To Buck he gives the pocket calculator he's never without. Even when he gives to his friends his heart and his mind on the way out of life, they aren't alerted. They don't go for help for him.

The novel dramatizes the classic warning signs of suicide. A novel is a more likely format for presenting them than a pamphlet that would go unread. I wrote it because this epidemic is largely silent. I never see the telephone numbers of local suicide hotlines on the bulletin boards of the schools I visit, not even in schools that have lost students. And the young go to those schools from homes where suicide is never mentioned *because we don't have that kind of problem in our family.*

In a deteriorating human condition there has to be a trigger. In *Remembering the Good Times* it's the school Trav attends, a burgeoning, impersonal high school superficially serving a rootless tract-house suburb. The school provides neither human shelter nor any real academic challenge, despite its guidance counselors, its P.R.-oriented administration, and its inevitable programs for the gifted. Already troubled, Trav opts for death because he doesn't believe he's being prepared for the challenges of adult life.

A major hazard in writing the novel was to oversimplify, to imply a clear grasp of all the anguish deep-rooted in Trav. If we knew all we need to know about what drives the young to destruction, we wouldn't have this epidemic on our hands. We write not what we know, but what we wonder about. A novel is about uncertainties.

But the warning signals of suicide are well documented and are enacted in the novel. As an adolescent Trav lives in a world of friends, school, and his own essential solitude. He keeps his distance from his own family, who are portrayed as characteristic, caring parents who see little of their son.

Yet as recently as this morning a letter comes from a young reader, congratulating me on a book about a boy driven to kill himself by his heartless mother and father. She'd overlooked much of the book, including this passage in Kate's voice:

> "When you're as uncomfortable with yourself as Trav is and you see the very same traits in your parents, then you just turn on them. You want to shift the blame onto them and get out from under it yourself."

By adolescence there are children so blinded by their anger at permissive parents that they will rewrite every book they read. The other recurring response is in the letter that says, "I love your book, but I didn't like the ending. The boy shouldn't have killed himself." Writers are confronted by the paradox of readers who love books they didn't like. They want tragedies with happy endings. They want a way out and believe there always is one.

This book, which I wrote for young people to read on their own, needs teaching. For one thing it needs to be read twice, because few readers come to the end knowing what it's about. They need to read again those messages Trav is sending to see them for what they are. The novel needs talking over, and I'm glad when the letters come from young people who've met Kate, Polly, Buck, and Trav in the classroom and are talking about the book with a teacher.

One of the first considerations in writing a novel, planning it, is viewpoint. Who's going to tell this story, in the full knowledge that the author can't? At first I thought Trav would have to tell it because his problems had distanced him so far from his closest friends. But that version became an extended suicide note, and few suicides leave notes. Besides, if he'd been able to express his fears, he might not have had to die.

I tried the novel from Kate's viewpoint. She's an articulate problem-solver, but readers are too likely to trivialize a story told by a girl about a boy as a romance. Buck became the narrator who has to survive a terrible loss without becoming the next statistic.

A suicide victim can't be a protagonist for young readers,

because the book must be the biography of a survivor. The novel can't end with Trav's death. It has to end at a new beginning as Kate and Buck learn how to move on without him. This becomes the heart of the matter, because Kate is a girl who's always believed that every problem has a solution, and Buck is a boy who hasn't given himself permission to cry.

Remembering the Good Times can't be the definitive treatment of an issue this widespread. It can't be about every victim or survivor. Its framework of friendship interrupted reckons without the young victim who kills himself because he has no friends.

While I was writing it, a real-life boy in an upstate New York town went to school one morning and told twelve of his seventh-grade classmates that he was going to kill himself. He went home that night and did it. He hadn't sent out signals. He'd delivered a clear statement of intent.

Afterward people went to those twelve students and said, "Why didn't you say something? Why didn't you sound the alarm?"

But they were American kids going through puberty. They don't communicate with adults. They don't have to.

And people said to them, "Did you know that in this community there are social agencies to help the despairing and the suicidal?" No, they'd never heard of them. They went to a school without the suicide-hotline number on the bulletin board. They came from homes where the subject never arose. They lived in a town not zoned for tragedy. Besides, the only government and community they acknowledged was one another. And so even a novel about a boy who kills himself has to be, somehow, better, more hopeful, than real life.

When *Remembering the Good Times* was published, I took copies to the suicide-hotline workers who had helped me in research. They were crestfallen. "But it's about a teenager," they said. "Now we're hearing from nine-year-olds."

Death is a thread that runs through these books. In *Father Figure* a mother's death forces the reunion between father and sons. A girl's death in *Close Enough to Touch* compels a boy to confront his own emotions. *Remembering the Good Times* is about a boy who dies.

We hear rumblings from various adult quarters about the preoccupation with death in young-adult books. There are even parents who confuse suicide with sex and think that if their children find out what it is, they'll want to try it. Death is one issue among many that ignite people who want childhood and even adolescence to be a refuge of innocence. "Why can't kids just be kids?" they ask, now that they know they can't be.

Their children confront death at closer range than many an adult ever has. They write about it in compositions. In my teaching days they often wrote about the loss of a grandparent in their need to get down on paper their first experience of death. Now they often write of an older brother or sister killed through drunk driving or killed by a drunk driver.

They know about drug overdoses and murder committed on school property. Just when we thought we'd banished death to the wings, just when no boy could imagine being required to die for his country, death took a giant step nearer the young, and they to it. Even in the twenty-first century AIDS still stalks the land, and the world. As the century turns, parents and parent groups continue the battle against medically accurate sex education in schools.

Before our books reach them, they've been media-implanted with the grotesques of film death. They've memorized movies I've never seen: *A Nightmare on Elm Street, New Jack City, Friday the 13th, The Blair Witch Project,* Texas chain saws, poltergeists, endless slasher flicks, a genre ominously called "Chicks in Chains," along with the commercialized mayhem of Saturday morning cartoons. Freddy Krueger is the baby-sitter now. In defense of television, the late Eric Sevareid once said that in many American homes it's the only coherent voice ever heard.

Vincent Canby identifies this blitz as another contribution of the riotous 1960's:

> Once the American film was liberated in 1968, when the Code was replaced by the rating system, Hollywood could match the yardage of naked flesh from abroad, with the extra added attraction of explicit violence, which had never much appealed to overseas movie makers.[1]

Now that the rented video has liberated the young from the ratings system, very young children see any film they want to see, if not in their own homes then in another.

Before our books reach our readers, heads have rolled. Blood

1. *The New York Times,* September 20, 1992.

flows freely on television, along with language that could get any faculty member but the coach fired. Journalism is more outspoken and graphic, too, in the era of the helicopter news crew and the handheld camera. Though the young, in their need for happy endings, aren't faithful viewers of the evening news, few avoid the repeated image of cops beating a suspect, of gang members dragging a passing truck driver out of the cab to shatter his skull and his life. Whether they can distinguish between real blood and blood as a theatrical prop, we can't be sure.

Young people urge us to vulgarize our work to keep pace with their taste for death as pop art. "Do you read any Christopher Pike?" their letters inquire. Whatever has been done to them by the gross-out imagery of death in their childhoods, the crucial moment comes after that. Teenagers don't believe they can die.

How else to explain the continued popularity of drunk driving? Proving his macho and her maturity, drunk as skunks behind the wheel, is a higher priority than anything to do with distant death. Death is something that happens to other people, the elderly and the unlucky. There's hard evidence that young people have committed suicide on Friday night in some sort of idea that they'd be back in school on Monday morning. After all, they've tested every rule; why not cheat death too? Adolescents aren't nearly as rational as we want them to be, and we lose them in pretending they are. They smoke more than we do too.

Television's promise of eternal life is that the actors gunned down and blown apart on the screen will live to play other roles. Can any book go head-to-head with the combined force of film power and teenagers' belief in their invincibility?

Only a very young writer or a crank believes his words will change people or the world. But we owe our readers a responsible exploration of death as one of the realities. It aligns with the underlying message of all our books, the hard-to-teach truth that in the long run you will be held responsible for the consequences of your actions. A thirteen-year-old murders his best friend, and so he gets to be on television. "I didn't kill him," he tells the camera. "The gun did."

We need more novels to ask the young what they think death is, as their nearest adults are increasingly powerless to save them. In the 1980's the chief killers of the young were suicide, drunk driving, and murder. They still are. Life keeps giving us new reasons to write about death.

CHAPTER NINE

And we get the ideas for our books from the letters of our readers. The mail delivery looms large when it brings the only human voice all day. It's eerie here in the writing room. You're growing older every minute while your readers remain the same age.

It's a rare reader who writes back, and so I scan every line and between them. Writing isn't self-expression, it's communication, and it works best when it's two-way.

Reader mail falls into two unequal categories. Most of the letters by far are assigned by teachers. We've all had this one: "Our teacher told us to write to our favorite author, and I'm the only one in the room writing to you."

And one I've pressed and preserved: "Our teacher told us to

write to our favorite author. Could you get me the address of Danielle Steel?"

The assigned letter is a somewhat good thing. After all, letter-writing is a dead art, murdered by the telephone in the child's room and the phone cards that accompany them to college, and the cell phone presently making a hell of every public place. Worse, now there's e-mail, the idiot stepchild of the well-composed letter on actual stationery sent at the stately pace of snail mail. Oddly, this old-fashioned letter is still being assigned by teachers, though they never seem to tell their students what a letter is and isn't. Most of the letters to the author are rough drafts, for the sound reason that their writers can get grades on rough drafts. But the assigned letter brings news from people who wouldn't have written otherwise, and evidence of which novels are being used in classrooms.

Then there are the letters from young people who wanted to write them. They often come in the summertime from people thoughtful enough, and lonely enough, to reach back. There's even the red-letter-day letter from someone who read almost the same book you wrote.

Most often they're from readers arrested by a single element. People read for the shock of recognition, and young readers seem more shockable. The mere mention of a McDonald's or a Wal-Mart in a book will bring forth the inquiry, "Do you live around here?" Alexander Armsworth and his friends attend Horace Mann School, and so letters come from Horace Mann schools around the country. When the best hostelry of Bluff City was revealed to be the Cornhusker Hotel, letters came for years from Lincoln, Nebraska. A book called *Unfinished Portrait of Jessica* enjoys a separate sale to people named Jessica.

Readers read to become the characters, and young people identify more intimately than the rest of us. "I am Blossom Culp," the letters sometimes say. I want them to become her, of course, but I could hardly hope they'd be willing.

They write to explain that you got the book all wrong; you forgot to finish it. You quit before the happy ending. "Where's the rest of it?" they ask. "Are you doing a sequel?"

In fact, they want a sequel for every book they approve of— a series. If there's one thing the young despise, it's novelty. Librarians report the young patron returning a book to say, "I want another one *exactly* like this one." They want every book, every part—every parent—to be the same. They issue the challenge to write a brand-new book for readers who need the certainty of the same old thing. Change is a threat, whatever its form. Television's regular programming wins again.

They stamp their idealism and post their hopes. People read fiction for the human relationships, and the belonging. Novels have stronger shapes than the worlds of the readers, stronger ties, and they want to climb into the book and live there. They want to read about and be survivors. Even a book fraught with cautionary messages, even terror, becomes a safer place than the reader's life. The snuffing and dismemberment of video games is a more comforting locale than middle school.

They don't just rewrite what they read; they reverse. The first letter about *Princess Ashley* said, "Chelsea and Ashley are just like me and my best bud." My hope that the reader will distinguish between friendship and obeying a conniving group leader is down the tubes in the first letter. They challenge in ways they never meant and bring you low with their approval. And you try again.

You throw them a lifeline, and they throw it back. A letter from a boy who read *Close Enough to Touch* in class says, "I'm only writing because I have to. There wasn't anything to the book. It was only about a guy's feelings." And you try again.

They write to tell you about this friend of theirs, and she has this mother who's loud and wears too much makeup. . . . They write about this girl who knows this boy, and he . . .

After *Remembering the Good Times* they write to say that the trouble with the book is that they didn't read it in time. They write things too painful and personal to repeat.

Some of the letters are illegible, and after eight years of schooling, a lot of people can't spell their hometown ("Philadelpilla"). A lot of people spell *a lot* "alot." In fact, all but a few do. People everywhere want you to know the names of their pets and wonder if you have any, and so cats and dogs, and the occasional lizard, stalk through my stories. Some write so politely that you realize the genteel tradition is not dead. Some write in an advanced state of camaraderie ("Richard, my man! How's it going?"). Some write from high school to say they used to read you when they were kids. You find that you love and are driven half berserk by people you will never meet.

And their letters turn you abruptly in new directions. The best of them give glimpses into the daily lives of the writers. Throughout the middle 1970's letters mentioned something they assumed I knew, and I didn't. The phrase recurred: "Today after school when we got to the mall . . ." Or more troubling: "Today at the mall . . ."

While I was deeply immured in the provincialism of Manhattan, the American shopping mall built for the convenience of adults who earned the money they spent was being co-opted by the young. I barely knew what a mall was, and it was hard to grasp that home was optional, school more optional still, but daily attendance at the mall was required. I tried not to notice. But it began to make a terrible kind of sense. The shopping mall is the only paved place in some suburbs, the only center. And it holds out the hope that you *can* buy the happiness promised by those twenty-three thousand commercials you've been watching since the beginning.

I put off these unwholesome thoughts as long as I could; then I grabbed up a notepad and headed for the Port Authority bus depot. The next thing I remember is standing in the parking lot of someplace called Paramas Park, New Jersey. A vision of hell. I went that day to the mall, where nothing but letters could have sent me, to shop for a novel.

It must have been at the mall when I truly learned at last that real life is too extreme for fiction. I interviewed shopkeepers who, like teachers and librarians, are on the firing line every day. I expected to hear that their chief problem was teenage shoplifters. They said a bigger problem was the parent dropping off the much younger child at nine in the morning and not coming back till nine at night. "We're into day care here," they said.

I drifted through the mall in the patterns of the young, on their heels. If an adult stranger taking notes had been haunting my adolescent peer group back when we hung out at Raycraft's drugstore, we'd have been out of there like shots. At the mall I noticed how invisible adults were growing to the young.

In my travels I dropped in on malls across the country, all those Gallerias and Fashion Valleys, where every day seemed to be a school holiday. The mall became metaphor for coming of age, suburban, consumerist, and climate-controlled, the place to buy your disguises where no adult is truly in charge.

Then it was time to write the novel. I wrote it the usual seven times and sat back pretty satisfied, until I reread it. I'd enjoyed writing it in a way, and that's a bad sign. Happy writing makes for sad reading. I'd written a sort of junior version of *The Decline of the West* right here at JCPenney. To call it a cautionary tale doesn't express it. Everybody died in the parking lot.

I'd been a little overheated in writing it, overresearched. Nobody likes too much bad news in a novel, and this was nothing but. I filed it in the fireplace, downcast that I hadn't been able to follow the generation of my readers where they'd gone.

For the next two years there were shopping-mall references everywhere I turned, in and out of the letters. A series of syndicated articles called "The Malling of America" appeared in newspapers nationwide. Driven back to the typewriter, I started over, beginning with tone.

I wrote a satire of life at the mall and of my own previous manuscript. I replaced the violence with adventure and tempered the menace with laugh lines. I wove in my recurring themes: the difference between friendship and peer grouping, the search for family. I called it *Secrets of the Shopping Mall*.

The hero and heroine of the piece are Barnie and Teresa, and they're in junior high, because she's taller than he is. In fact, he has a disability. He's too smart for seventh grade and too short for eighth. They're escapees from the inner city where they've defied their local gang leader, a comic villain named Harley Probst, main man of the King Kobras. They flee for their lives and can never return. Novels are about people who have to move forward because they can't go back.

At the end of the suburban bus line they find themselves at thinly disguised "Paradise Park," a place that astonishes them as much as it had astonished me. They enter the mall near closing time and take cover in the beds-and-bedding department of the major store. Beneath a candlewick-covered queen-size, Barnie suggests the scope of the story ahead.

> "Well, look at it this way. A big store like this is a total life-support system, right? I figure we can settle in for quite a while, if we don't get caught."
>
> "Like for how long?" Teresa wonders.
>
> "Quite a while," Barnie tells her. "Till we're grown."

And so Barnie and Teresa act out the fond fantasy of many a reader, to move permanently into the mall, cutting all other ties, to come of age there. They learn to pass unnoticed during the day and to take cover by night. They forage in the deli. They become suburban pioneers on what I think will be the last American frontier. Why go to the moon when you can get to the mall?

But the word *secrets* is in the title, and so the novel must deliver. As it happens, Barnie and Teresa aren't alone as mall stowaways. They were spotted the moment they walked in and have been monitored since, and not by the night watchman or the plainclotheswoman or any adult.

They've stumbled onto the domain of a peer group of perfect, preppie suburban kids, run away from the rigors of permissive homes and elective school and reorganized under the iron rule of a peer-group leader in the mall as a sort of mother house. And she's no leather-bound Harley Probst. She's a poisonously sweet, perfectly groomed dominatrix named Barbie. Her consort is a flawless boy in a blue blazer, inevitably named Ken.

On the terrible night after hours when these "Store People" apprehend Barnie and Teresa in the junior miss department, Barbie introduces them, bound and gagged, to this new world.

"You're on our turf," she murmured, still smiling. "You have absolutely no rights whatever. Because you are not one of us."

The girl looked all the way down the length of Teresa, and her eyes drifted over to Barnie's lumber jacket. "We will dispose of you," the girl went on, "in any way we choose. But we are very fair, and everyone in our little . . . society is an equal. Except of course for me. I am more equal than the others. But you two—" Her terrifying, glittering gaze swept over Barnie again, though it was really Teresa she was giving the business to, "are not our equals at all."

Will Barnie and Teresa find salvation in the suburbs by assuming the correct uniform and becoming good soldiers in Barbie's occupation of the mall? Hardly. Tough-minded Teresa refers to

Barbie and Ken's group as a bunch of "night-blooming Nazis," but they give her pause. They give me pause. And the essential similarity between the rules of inner city and the peer patterns of suburbia is a lightly buried message. The fact that young readers aren't ready to believe that one gang is very like another is one more reason to make the point.

Barnie and Teresa have to do more than maintain the integrity of their friendship. They have to bring Barbie down. Novels are about people who have no choice but to act. This novel isn't about a mall at all, though Paradise Park plays its part as readers' setting of choice. It's about the separate totalitarian society the young set up anywhere they can, about the search for a punitive leader. *Time* magazine called the book "A Lord—and Taylor—of the Flies."[1]

Secrets of the Shopping Mall wasn't my first comedy, but it was the first one recast from a tragedy. From that experience I learned a basic truth. Humor is anger that was sent to finishing school.

I'd already written a novel on an issue of high seriousness that I, at least, thought could profit from humorous treatment. *Representing Super Doll* is a comedy on that pressing adolescent question: How attractive am I to the opposite sex?

The young still believe as we did that beautiful people are spared the problems of mere mortals. *Representing Super Doll* is therefore about the most beautiful girl on earth, because I say so. She cannot lose a beauty contest.

Though she starts out low as Miss Hybrid Seedcorn, she's

1. "Packaging the Facts of Life," August 23, 1982.

headed for the top. In fact, she wins so many beauty contests, she hardly has a friend left. And where do we get the ideas for our novels? I got the idea for this one while waiting backstage to go on a television talk show. I was trapped back there for three hours with Miss Teenage America's mother. After that experience I thought God owed me a novel.

But the readers of *Representing Super Doll* didn't bombard me with demands for a sequel. The readers of *Secrets of the Shopping Mall* did, and for more than a decade. But I thought I'd told the story and exploited the mall as setting. People sent clippings of mall news too.

Some from Edmonton, Alberta, and Bloomington, Minnesota, were about how malls were growing to science-fictional size. But apparently there was trouble in Paradise. The clippings began to chronicle the decline of this empire. An image arose of abandoned malls like Roman ruins, windswept and decaying at the edge of town. They had overbuilt, but there was another factor. A hair-raising clipping came from an Ohio newspaper about a mall that had been so thoroughly vandalized by its teenage patrons that it had been forced into bankruptcy. Most of what they had done to their setting of choice was barely printable and a mile too extreme for fiction.

I wrote another novel. It's not a sequel, but it is a satire, called *Bel-Air Bambi and the Mall Rats*. In this one nobody takes up full-time residence at the mall. It's no longer habitable, or even in business.

The story is about a high-flying Hollywood TV producer's family who go over budget once too often. One day these show-biz kids, Bambi, Buffie, and their little brother, Brick, are being chauffeured to select private schools in West Los Angeles. The next day the whole family's on the lam, wiped out and retreating to the rustic middle-American town where Dad grew up. They even find themselves enrolled at the school he once attended—a public school.

> Just last Monday, we'd been having lunch out on the lanai at the Stars of Tomorrow School: diet seltzer and designer pasta. Now, Thursday, we'd just been through the steam table at Hickory Fork Consolidated. The smart money packed their lunch and bought milk. Off our turf, Bambi and I ended up with mystery-meat sandwiches on white bread, mashed potatoes, and Jell-O that fought back.

As with all satires, it's the world turned upside down. In this one the California show-business family appears to be the only cohesive unit in sight. The rest of Dad's bucolic hometown is fragmented and falling apart. The coach-run school is dominated by a countrified gang, whose molls are a ragged line of out-of-shape cheerleaders. This peer group is ruled by an unpromising figurehead named Jeeter and the power behind his throne, a villainess aptly named Tanya Hyde. Bambi and her sister, Buffie, cross her path when they mistakenly visit the high-school girls' rest room.

> There was an explosion then, from behind us. I'd been hearing them all day. And sounds like distant gunfire. But this was one of the doors to the stalls banging back, and echoing. I saw it all in the mirror. The fog of blue smoke in the stall,

and this extra-tall girl stepped out of there, in plastic leather, ripped denim, white snakeskin boots. She was all black and white like an old movie. She had a year's supply of eyeliner and about four pounds of matted hair, shoe-polish black. Pretty impressive and the scariest-looking girl I'd ever seen.

Bel-Air Bambi and the Mall Rats is a story of a family who find a unity they'd never quite needed where they came from. It's about young characters who have to go forward because they can't go back. And while they're about it, they have to clean up Dad's Clintonian hometown to return it to some approximation of his memories.

At the edge of town is the mall that Jeeter and Tanya's Mall Rat gang has put off limits to the adults so they can use it as their power base. Naturally Bambi and Buffie are going to have to beard the Mall Rats in their ruined den.

Things were entirely too quiet. A moving moon skated reflectively across the truck's hood. The mall's main entrance was a big mouth, with a loose board over a kicked-in door. "I wonder if they're bright enough to post a guard," Bambi whispered.

"Let's not find out. Let's—"

But she edged up and flattened her back against the boards. She was playing one of her roles—urban girl guerrilla or something. Then she was gone, swallowed by the mall. My heart hammered. But I followed her inside.

The mall as setting and metaphor is ripe for satire and may yet see a third treatment. After all, it's that world turned upside down where children enjoy a higher standard of living than their own parents, one more reason not to grow up. The children of the desolate inner city are hung with embarrassing quantities of gold jewelry, and they pay more for shoes than we do. The suburban school parking lot is ranked with the late models of people whose parents are carpooling. The phrase "I'd kill for a leather jacket like that one" is no longer hyperbole.

Not all their income is unearned. Malls depend on staffing by teenagers who work to support their cars. The young will mortgage the future to pay for the present every chance they get. Many of them would prefer a car to a high-school education, now that they have that choice.

Materialism is one more massive way in which coming of age has been pulled out of shape. But nobody they know queries the young about what they're really charging their parents for, or what they really think they can buy.

Secrets of the Shopping Mall is spiky with the status-seeking of a generation more brand-conscious than conscious. *Bel-Air Bambi and the Mall Rats* pits the togetherness of family against a community knuckled under to a youth gang. When you write satire for seventh-graders, you have some explaining to do. They don't all grasp the barbs at consumerism run amok. And satire runs hard to keep pace with their realities. Many a real-life daughter forbids her mother to appear at the mall in case they might encounter each other there. But novels rush in where parents fear to tread.

Not every novel can be a comedy. Some issues forbid it. Some stories, like *Those Summer Girls I Never Met,* walk that line between laughter and tears. But as a teacher I'd thought that young people could laugh away half their problems if they would or knew how. Classroom laughter rose chiefly from nervousness or derision, and they always laughed at others, never at themselves. The occasional true comedians were almost worth the trouble they gave you.

"Seriousness is the refuge of the shallow," Rita Mae Brown writes.[1] Comedy and satire march in a proud, age-old tradition. Yet a barrier for books is that they don't include laugh tracks to cue response. It becomes a high calling to try to convince the young that real comedy doesn't need a laugh track, that in and out of books, humor can be the shortest trip to the truth.

1. *Starting from Scratch: A Different Kind of Writers' Manual,* Bantam, 1988.

CHAPTER TEN

It was teaching that made a writer out of me. I'd be a teacher still, had I been allowed to teach as I'd been taught. But it was some other profession when I got there. My generation of teachers were never to find a substitute for learning based on the bedrock of literacy and delayed gratification, but we tried. We initiated the minicourse to fit the unstretched attention span, and grade inflation to flatter those we couldn't control. Audio-visual aids were going to save our bacon in one era, computers in another.

We turned away from rote learning because Jean Piaget said, "We need to cultivate bright minds, not memories."[1] We

1. *Phi Delta Kappan,* March 1966.

read Jane Howard's *Please Touch* and set up T-groups for faculty sensitivity training. We had qualified hopes for *Sesame Street* as a surrogate preschool parent, but John Holt didn't like the program because it was "full of little lesson plans."[1]

We introduced bilingualism and threw out Latin in a confusing double play. We tried humanities-based curricula, career education, the Discovery Method, performance contracting, the open classroom—all this a generation before whole language and multiculturalism.

And the kids got us all wrong. Schools and standards became elective in ways we never meant. We introduced remedial programs to level the playing field, and they saw them as alternatives to homework. Their idea of modular scheduling was to cut first period. We devised the gifted program to provide the willing student with some approximation of the regular classroom of thirty years before.

When teachers got sensitive, the students went shopping. While we scrambled to find innovative alternatives to our own authority, the students began to vanish before our very eyes into their private lives, in pursuit of tougher leaders. By the time we got to team teaching, we nearly outnumbered them. While we bombed, private schools boomed.

But we certainly had more varied careers than our own teachers. We may even have come to know our students better than our teachers had known us. When teachers were no longer the chief authority figures in classrooms, the students turned less carefully composed faces our way. Wanting parents, they cast

1. *The Atlantic Monthly,* May 1971.

us as theirs. Though their vocabularies were smaller, they didn't mince words with us.

But through all the changes, one truth came clear. These altered beings were the young people we, too, would have been, had it been allowed. They became the people I wanted to write for. I carried them home in my head.

Once I'd decided to quit teaching, I meant to do a quiet vanishing act. It wasn't the sort of faculty that gave going-away parties, and I've never heard from them since. But I found I couldn't go wordlessly away. In the last class of the last day, I looked out at the room and seemed to see it for the first time.

The students sat in the warring camps of both puberty and New York City. Here the group of black students. There the Puerto Rican students. Across from them the Jewish students. And down front right under my nose, the lone Lutheran from Staten Island, the only one who took notes.

I said to them what was in my mind, even my heart. "If I seated you the way you seat yourselves, I would be fired." Then I closed my roll book for the last time.

After class one student hung back. She was the class sophisticate, so heaven alone knows what ever became of her. She came up to my desk and said softly, "I just want you to know that what you said in class today was in the *worst possible taste*." Then she darted away to catch up with her group.

That we had ever expected teenagers of all people to create a utopian society was naive at best. It ranked right down there with reading readiness. To expect the young to defy their own psychologies in order to enact our political theories disfigured them and their education. At the least we owed them safety in the new patterns we tried to impose on them. They became more biased against people beyond their groups than we had been, more frightened, and it wasn't a phase, a period of adjustment. We know that now.

But a career in writing isn't an escape from anything. The novel has opportunities denied the teacher, and television. Unlike film, a novel need not brand the race or ethnicity of its characters unless it wants to. A novel can begin at the next epidermal layer down, to explore what we all have in common.

Publishing turned out to be politicized too, but it is a novel's obligation to be politically incorrect. A novel is about the individual, not the group, and politics is not only the enemy of art, it's the enemy of the individual.

The minute I left teaching, I missed it. Bells no longer divided the day into manageable time slots. For a writer, there is no faculty lounge where you can go on your free period to practice choral primal screaming. For a writer, there's nobody around to blame.

I wrote a first novel and maybe two more by keeping my own students in mind: the rhythms of their speech, what they'd responded to in reading, and what they hadn't. I wrote, trying to catch glimpses of their faces on the blank pages in the typewriter.

But their faces began to fade, and their voices echoed away into silence. I seemed to recall how they changed their protective coverings every semester or so, and I noticed time was passing, even without the bells. I was soon out again, looking for ideas in other people's classrooms in author-in-the-school programs. These lightning raids remain the chief source of the ideas for my books.

I was to visit schools and libraries in places, even countries, where I'd never been. As a teacher I'd learned the least from my students by what they said and the most by what they'd written, safe from the hearing of their powerful peers. The voices in those pages still ring in mine. Now, before I visit students in schools, I ask their teachers to assign compositions and mail them to me in advance. That request eliminates some invitations, but I believe in it.

Reading those papers before we meet gives me glimpses of the students ahead of time. I can write some notes of encouragement in the margins. After all, they go to schools where they'll never win letter sweaters for literacy. Then when we meet, we meet as fellow writers, not as speaker and audience.

The paper I ask the students to write is entitled:

SOMETHING THAT HAPPENED TO ME
THAT WOULD FIT INTO A NOVEL

If there were a foolproof writing assignment, we'd have heard about it by now, but this one casts a broad net. The papers sometimes reveal their writers' expectations for fiction, what they think stories are. The writing forges a link between the self and the story, and it sharpens the eye for the material at hand near their lives. I hope they see from their classmates' papers that something really does happen around here.

It's an assignment that might invite self-involved self-expression, but most of the papers are about other people. Often they write about themselves in childhood, preserving their present privacy. They are more preoccupied with siblings older and younger than I'd noticed as a teacher. No paper ever touches on the peer-group power structure running their schools, because some subjects are too touchy to treat. Sex and drugs are never mentioned. In Alaska you get a lot of stories about fish that got away and the night the bear got on the roof. In California, a lot about life in the aftermath of parental divorce. The most popular settings coast-to-coast are the mall and the houses where they're baby-sitting.

One in two hundred is a comic tale, written by a boy. One in ten is a hard-to-credit revision of a Harlequin romance, by a girl. Then there are the people who won't play fair. There are eighth-grade boys who write science fiction—by the yard. Something that happened to *them* that would fit into a novel? No, but they're in the depths of puberty, and they aren't talking. Stories to them are only for escape, and the farther the better. Their silences are as telling as their words, and I'm moved to write what they won't.

When our roles reverse and they're writing for me, it sets up a dialogue. They're no longer the critical consumers they are at the mall, in front of the TV, and in the daily classroom. The experience of writing something that doesn't go directly to the teacher and nowhere else gives the project life. Even sending it through the mail is an innovation.

Then, suddenly, a paper will leap out of the pack and give me a new novel to write. I wrote a novel called *Unfinished Portrait of Jessica* inspired by a paper entitled "Something That

Happened to Me That Would Fit into a Novel," written by a girl in a town, somewhere:

When I was three years old, my dad left me and my mom. He and my mother had always fought, but it was a great surprise to me when he left. You know, I thought they'd always be together. Of course that was only a three-year-old's point of view, but for some reason I think I'd still feel the same way if it happened now.

I don't remember much about them being together. What I do remember is locked in my memory. I remember one Christmas when I got a stick-horse and a cowgirl outfit. I rode that horse everywhere. I think that was the Christmas before he left.

The day he left, I had been listening to them argue. I guess my dad was stressed out and my mom was just a bitch. Now I see that, but then I thought I had done something wrong. I thought I was to blame.

I was crying and screaming, "Daddy, please don't go," when he walked out the door. I followed him out and clung to his leg until he got to the car. This was when he pried me off his leg, jumped in the car, and sped off. He wouldn't even look me in the eye, and he didn't say good-bye. I guess I can understand why now. He knew that if he looked at me standing there, left all alone, he wouldn't be able to go. After all, he needed to leave.

I thought that I was to blame until I was about nine years old. At nine is when I moved in with my dad. Everything was perfect until my dad met my stepmother. She and my daddy eloped and before you knew it, she was my step-mother. She envied the attention Dad gave me. She was the type of stepmother to be in *Cinderella*. She still is.

Now my dad is a stranger. My stepmom has gotten some sort of hold on him. She's a psychologist, and therefore she feels like she can solve all the problems of the world. She and my father have a booklet on how to parent and everything. Obviously, whoever wrote the booklet doesn't know a thing about parenting, because the booklet is not helping.

Well, now they've more or less run me out of the house with their rules and booklets and insincerity. I'm not liv-ing with them now. (Did I happen to mention that?) I've left my dad, just like he left me, but at least I said good-bye.

Sometimes you get more than you bargained for. That paper burned with an emotion conspicuously absent from the other papers. I couldn't put it aside. Individual lines haunted me. "I guess my dad was stressed out and my mom was just a bitch."

In the margin I wrote back, "Why is Dad being let off easier than Mom? He was the one who left."

And another line: "[My stepmother] envied the attention Dad gave me."

In the margin I wrote back, "Could there be envy on both sides?"

My heart went out to that stepmother. How many steppar-ents out there realize they've been set up for failure? How many are looking for guidebooks, hoping they'll work, in an age when a child's anger takes precedence over an adult's needs?

But the whole paper is there in the first line, where it should be. "When I was three years old, my dad left me and my mom."

It's a sorrow when very young children feel they've been divorced. But when a girl is willing to forgive her departing father and punish her remaining mother, a question arises that a novel can ask.

Yet a novel can't arise directly from this student's piece of very real writing. A novel is the chronicle of change. We dare never leave our main characters on the last page where we found them on the first. The girl who wrote her story is still shifting blame. She was a senior in high school, and it seemed to me she was just about to walk into an adult world where all women are the enemy, all men are just walking out the door, and she is herself only a victim, however hostile.

Her teacher was interested in this paper too. Privately I asked her, "She left her mother to live with her father. Then she left her father. Is she homeless now?"

"Of course not," the teacher said. "She went straight back to her mother. She just doesn't want to admit it."

And so it was time for a novel.

Unfinished Portrait of Jessica is the story of a fourteen-year-old girl whose father leaves her and her mother, and so it's a novel about nearly half of my readers. They know more about divorce than I do. In the story Jessica watches her father walk away, and the minute he's out the door, he's perfect.

> He wasn't like other people's boring fathers, who went off in
> the morning in suits and brought work home every night.
> Blacksocked fathers in Brooks Brothers suits, who did things

at desks. My dad wore a flight jacket, and when he went away the world stopped . . .

Jessica turns then in rage on her mother for not being woman enough to hold him.

Is it rational to turn on the one parent you have left? But Jessica is fourteen, and she's lost the first man she ever loved. A fourteen-year-old American girl will punish her mother anyway, even without divorce, and Jessica's mother takes a lot of abuse. Then Jessica's mother says something she might not have said in real life, and she says it very much against her better judgment. At the end of her patience she asks her daughter if she'd like to spend the Christmas holidays with her dad, in Mexico. Jessica believes it's a miracle. She believes her mother can no longer keep them apart. She even believes her dad has sent for her. She goes to him planning never to return.

Mexico: I saw this unknown place alive and beckoning across the blank door to the living room. Endless beach under a white sun. I saw Dad and me, only the two of us in the world, walking along the beach, and my profile was turned up to him. We walked hand in hand, and I felt the grit of sand in his strong grip and the cool surf between my toes as it scalloped the sand. I felt Mexico warm on my face and tried to erase the days between.

In all my books, young characters take trips to learn things they couldn't have learned at home. Jessica's journey is more educational than most. The major setting is Acapulco, where her father has gone in pursuit of the sun and of his own youth and, of course, in pursuit of another woman. But Jessica is fourteen, and she thinks her dream is within reach. She'll have him and Mom won't. She comes home early.

The story is told by a much older Jessica, looking back at the anger and confusion of her fourteenth year, the year Dad left and she tried to follow.

In real life she could go on being fourteen forever, the relationship with her mother unrepaired. She could go through life looking for her elusive father in every man she meets. She could be a professional victim. But a novel is the chronicle of change. The protagonist of a novel not only learns a truth, but acts on it.

Dealing with your loyalties in the aftermath of your parents' divorce isn't the work of a moment or a problem to be solved over the Christmas holidays. But a novel for the young is the story of a step, one step nearer maturity, even in an age when maturing itself has become an elective.

The book is called an unfinished portrait because all of our books are, and so are all of our readers.

Whatever the sources of our inspiration, our stories are all family stories. Barbie, as monster-mother figure undercover at the mall. Jessica's father always out of reach and younger in ways than his own daughter. Jim in *Father Figure* trying to be a dad to fill the void of not having one. And in a country awash with children set adrift and in need of foster care, Molly in *Strays Like Us,* looking for family and home among strangers. Whole family units, too, hanging in there together in a changing world: Verna Henderson's farm family in *Representing Super Doll*, the show-business Babcocks in *Bel-Air Bambi and the Mall Rats*. And in the comic fantasy of *Voices After Midnight*, a very modern family who discover their roots without meaning to when they come face-to-face with their own ancestors.

We celebrate and investigate the family in all its changing forms, trying to keep hard on the heels of reality, or at least within sight. We create fictitious characters who invite young readers to see family members as human beings. We portray families we didn't meet in the Dick and Jane primers. Isabelle Holland's superb *Of Love and Death and Other Journeys*. Bette Greene's *Summer of My German Soldier*. Pam Conrad's *Taking the Ferry Home*. M. E. Kerr's jarring *Gentlehands* and her *The Son of Someone Famous*. Paul Zindel's *The Effect of Gamma Rays on Man-in-the-Moon Marigolds*. Chris Crutcher's priceless short story "A Brief Moment in the Life of Angus Bethune":[1]

> Four parents are what I have all together, not unlike a whole lot of other kids. But quite unlike a whole lot of other kids, there ain't a hetero among 'em. My dad's divorced and remarried and my mom's divorced and remarried, so my mathematical account of my family suggests simply another confused teenager from a broken home. But my dads aren't married to my moms. They're married to each other. Same with my moms.

Even Angus's name is an indignity.

1. From *Connections: Short Stories by Outstanding Writers for Young Adults*, edited by Donald R. Gallo, Delacorte, 1989.

"Angus is a cow," I complained to my stepmother, Bella, the day in first grade I came home from school early for punching the bearer of this sad information in the stomach.

"Your mother must have had a good reason for naming you that," she said.

"For naming me after a cow?"

"You can't go around punching everyone who says that to you," she warned.

"Yes, I can," I said.

"Angus is a cow," I said to my mother when she got home from her job at Westhead Trucking Firm. "You guys named me after a cow."

"Your father's uncle was named Angus," she said, stripping off her outer shirt with a loud sigh, then plopping into her easy chair with a beer, wearing nothing but her bra; a bra, I might add, that could well have floated an ejected fighter pilot to safety.

Though our greatest challenge may lie in humanizing the American mother in the eyes of the American daughter— *Princess Ashley, Unfinished Portrait of Jessica,* Judy Blume's *Tiger Eyes*—we trace the perilous father-son relationship, too, from S. E. Hinton's *Tex* to Gary Paulsen's *The Haymeadow.* In Marc Talbert's *The Purple Heart* a boy anticipates a hero in his father's return from Vietnam and instead encounters a shattered man. In Graham Salisbury's *Blue Skin of the Sea* a boy's childhood is buffered and sustained by the abiding love of a father.

Sonny Mendoza in Salisbury's book also has the absolute love of his Hawaiian Aunty Pearl. Our books reach out for extended family. Billy and his uncle Wes in Ron Koertge's *The Arizona Kid*. Dicey Tillerman's search for a home in the person of an unknown grandmother in Cynthia Voigt's *Homecoming*. *Those Summer Girls I Never Met* is another of my portrayals of the elderly character as pivotal in the lives of the young.

It's the story of two teenagers, the children of a single suburban parent whom they hold in tight control. Drew Wingate, the narrator, wants but one thing from his sixteenth summer. At dawn on his birthday he wants that driver's license in his hands. If he doesn't get it on the first day, he's going to know that's where the rest of his life went wrong.

Drew has a younger sister, Steph. At fourteen she's nowhere near even a learner's permit, but she has her summer all mapped out too. She wants ninety uninterrupted days at the mall of her choice.

But the grandmother they hardly know sends for them to spend two endless weeks under her jurisdiction, on a European cruise. The grandchildren are almost speechless; they can think of no use for a grandparent whatever.

In real life they'd refuse the cruise and have the summers they want, and so in September they'd be just a little younger than they were in June. But books are better than real life, or we wouldn't have them. In the book they go on the cruise because their grandmother (and I) say so.

She isn't the grandmother they'd been introduced to in the picture books of early childhood: the white-haired, apple-cheeked lady in the big apron, baking cookies from scratch on a black iron stove down on the farm. She's nothing like that.

She's Connie Carlson, a Big Band singer left over from the 1940's, trying to keep her career afloat by doing shows for cruise-ship passengers.

She doesn't sing a grandmother's lullabies. She sings "Take the A Train" and "I'm in the Mood for Love." She's never worn an apron. She wears platform shoes and glossy black wigs and theatrical makeup.

> She smiles a little. Above the painted-on lips the skin is accordion pleated in fine wrinkles, but her cheeks are smooth, powdered. "I'm lucky to be working at all. I'm sixty-four years old. And I may have knocked off a couple of years."
>
> She plants her little fists on her sides. "Ancient?"
>
> ". . . Ah, oh, no," I say. Suave.
>
> "Sure it is. In this business a girl singer's ancient at *thirty*-four. That makes me prehistoric. I knew Dinah Shore before Holly Farms chicken. I knew Doris Day when her name was Kappelhoff. I knew Sinatra with hair."

This grandmother is in business for herself, and her grandchildren didn't know adults were. The only adults they'd ever known were serving them.

Their cruise is a voyage of discovery. In their grandmother, Drew and Steph catch glimpses of their own adult futures and their roots. In this experience they'd have avoided if they could, they find family. And the story is told as a comedy, because in the end it's too sad to tell in any other way.

Where do the ideas for our books come from, and the characters to tell them? Through observation—the kids in the coffee shop where I go every morning before settling down at the desk. Kids organizing one another every morning and not noticing me, because we gather our best research when nobody knows we're there. Kids in the coffee shop, endangering my health with their secondhand smoke, saying, "Anybody going to first period?"

The ideas come through the mail. *Our teacher told us to . . . Do you live around here? . . . I know this girl and she . . . Where's the sequel?*

We have to go out and get our ideas, dig like archaeologists for our artifacts in the schools and libraries and malls where our readers are. Lucky for us that they're all institutionalized so we can find them.

In our lonely work, we get our ideas from our colleagues. William Zinsser says:

> Writing is learned by imitation. I learned to write mainly by reading writers who were doing the kind of writing I wanted to do and by trying to figure out how they did it. S. J. Perelman told me that when he was starting out he could have been arrested for imitating Ring Lardner.[1]

And we get our ideas from Huckleberry Finn, who still gives us permission to look at the world through the eyes of the young.

We write our family stories in all the voices we can find,

1. *Writing to Learn*, Harper & Row, 1988.

except our own. Young voices, though of course we have to play all the parts, *be* all these people. I'm careful with my portrayals of adults: parents, grandparents, stepparents. In my books stepparents aren't going to be villainous, because the young are too likely to do that casting themselves. Parents aren't going to be perfect, but they aren't going to be stereotypes. They're going to be portrayed as whole human beings with their own needs.

But we don't write our novels in parental voices and better never try it. I've only written once in the voice of a parent. I call it:

Notes for the Refrigerator Door

No, my darling child,
You won't be going out again tonight.
If you have no homework, see me and we'll find some . . .
Math, perhaps, to help count the hours and the dollars
That slip so easily through your fingers;
Vocabulary, perhaps . . . you know?

But no, you won't be going out again tonight.
You're still a member of this family,
And it's a greater comfort to you than you know,
You know?

No, my darling child,
I don't owe you a car.
I know that public transportation is both bad and beneath you

And that your friends judge you by what you have,
But no, I don't owe you a car.
I know you're the best driver in the world.
And you'll get even better with practice,
But you'd wreck a car you were given
For reasons too obscure for you to know.

No, my darling child,
I won't be paying for your liquor,
However deeply buried this expenditure within
Your budget of necessities.

I know everybody who counts will get wasted this weekend,
And I know you can hold your liquor
And will get even better with practice,
But I'll be at home soberly awaiting your return,
So, no, I won't be paying for your liquor.

No, my darling child,
I don't understand.
One glimpse inside your school locker would leave me gaping
With amazement,
And I was never young myself.
I was born with this mortgage and this annoying capacity
To nag and care,
But I said yes to you too early and too often,
Hoping to convey my love,
Thinking that freedom would lead you toward responsibility,
And so, now: no.

And no, my darling child,
You can't come back home to live after you've finished college,
But then you won't have to if I say no often enough now.

And . . . P.S.
No, my darling child.
You can't charge it.

CHAPTER ELEVEN

It's the first day of school in New York City, an untried teacher's first day of grade-school teaching. Forty first-graders explode into her room. More than half of them speak no English. None of them have ever sat down. Some of them are hungry. Forty first-graders, and the mother of one of them.

She strides to the new teacher's desk with a printout from a religious cult. This mother's child may not pledge allegiance to the flag or to anything else. In this public-school classroom there can be no celebration or decoration for any holiday, national or religious. One mention of Halloween can cost this teacher her job, or her safety.

In leaving teaching, I wasn't destined to walk away from this either. Whatever you write, there are people who wish you wouldn't. Parents who expect higher standards than their own from teachers are among the earliest figures in American history. Censorship is as old as the word, and never better organized than now.

It never arises from a majority, not even the Moral one. As Ray Bradbury points out:

> Fire-Captain Beatty, in my novel *Fahrenheit 451,* described how the books were burned first by minorities, each ripping a page or a paragraph from this book, then that, until the day came when the books were empty and the minds shut and the libraries were closed forever.[1]

It's somehow cold comfort to reflect that a banning puts us up there with *The Adventures of Huckleberry Finn, The Grapes of Wrath, Watership Down, Ordinary People, The Catcher in the Rye, All Quiet on the Western Front, Where the Wild Things Are, Brave New World,* and *The American Heritage Dictionary.*

In the *Hartford Courant* Donald R. Gallo cites the removal of the following readings from a Connecticut school district: *The Chocolate War* "because it views females as sex objects, contains scenes of masturbation and cigarette smoking and includes offensive language." Robert Newton Peck's *A Day No Pigs Would Die* "because it's gory and deals with death." Paul Zindel's *The Pigman* "because of disrespect for parents and teachers, lack of consequences for inappropriate student behavior (drinking, smoking, stealing) and the absence of good role models." *Summer*

---

1. Quoted in Jo Ellen Ham's "Teenagers' Reading: Our Selection or the Censors'?" *Forum,* 1988.

of My German Soldier "because of offensive language, an abusive father and offensive situations." One of Robert Cormier's short stories, "In the Heat,"[1] "because of offensive vocabulary, a focus on death of a parent and the kind of role models portrayed."[2]

I began to appear on such lists because of Blossom Culp, of all people. While not meaty enough for the jaded tastes of young Stephen King and video-game addicts, Blossom's comic adventures have placed her and me on the forbidden-book list of a powerful wave of censors splendidly organized nationwide.

The author of my woes may well be Phyllis Schlafly. In one of her syndicated Copley News Service columns headlined "Where Have All the Good Old Books for Adolescents Gone? Schools force students to read dreary and depressing material," she condemns both *Ghosts I Have Been* and *The Ghost Belonged to Me,* warning that "the books could lead children to believe that, in order to be an interesting person, one should try to contact the dead and seek acquaintances who do likewise."

The young spur us on to conform to their taste, formed early by television's terminators, while certain parents, perhaps their own, attack the books and textbooks of library and school. The link is clear. When you cannot control your child's screen-time addiction, or your child, you have need of scapegoats.

More than any previous generation, parents now have reason to fear the loss of control of their children and the loss of their children's innocence. But they didn't lose that control to books.

---

1. From *Sixteen: Short Stories by Outstanding Writers for Young Adults,* Delacorte Press, 1984.
2. *Hartford Courant,* March 10, 1991.

Books aren't that powerful, and their children aren't that innocent. The sinking literacy rate plays its own role. When your child isn't achieving, a face-saver is to attack the book and the textbook. We would be much nearer nirvana now if parents feared schools more and their own children less.

One of the current tidal waves is impelled by the coordinated efforts of fundamentalist religious leaders with political aspirations. Astonishingly, here in the dawn of the twenty-first century there are people who will equate religious belief with the rankest kind of superstition, believing that ghost stories, Halloween decorations, and Ouija boards are secretly encoded, luring the young directly to devil worship. It's sorry evidence of our educational system's failure with the generation who are now parents. Only the nonreader fears books.

The fact that some of the superstars of the fundamentalist clergy have now been brought ludicrously low, and on television, has sent the movement in the local direction.

Textbook literature anthologies have been under particular fire. They make for a significant target considering that most young people don't use the library. Diane Ravitch says:

> Today's textbooks have a far lower intellectual content than those of the past. In Tennessee, the Holt series was criticized for including "The Wizard of Oz"—it allegedly teaches witchcraft and magic—and Anne Frank's diary—for allegedly suggesting that all religions are equally valid.[1]

---

1. "Where Have All the Classics Gone? You Won't Find them in Primers," *The New York Times Book Review,* May 17, 1989.

Nor are the foot soldiers in these local movements limited to impoverished people living on the outskirts of Southern towns. The statisticians tell us that while the membership of "mainline" churches continues a nationwide decline, fundamentalist churches burgeon.[1] The membership is rising through the social and economic class structure. A community was recently stymied by a prominent doctor's wife who checked out every book about Halloween in every branch library in town and refused to return them.

I was invited by a school librarian to speak to junior-high students and their parents during a young writers' workshop. One of the mothers refused to allow her son to read a book of mine on the reading list. That might have been as independent an act as she wished to make it seem, in spite of the fact that the book happened to be one of the titles cited in the Schlafly column. But then the mother granted an interview to the newspaper of the nearest big city and received prominent coverage. She made a public plea to keep me from appearing in the community.

Friends of mine sent me the clipping. Otherwise I would have shown up thinking my role was to encourage young writers, not to defend my books and my own menacing presence. I thought it was time for a phone call to the librarian who'd invited me. "You must have been very surprised by being attacked for a book like that," she said.

I wasn't. I was only surprised that a school librarian could be astonished by the attack this far along in the history of the

---

1. See "The Church Search," *Time,* April 5, 1993.

trend—astonished and unprepared. But it was a rich, picture-perfect, it-can't-happen-here kind of suburb. Fortunately I'd been forewarned, because the first junior-high student I encountered there asked me how I felt about the situation.

Apart from never volunteering the information to me in advance so that I could inform my publisher, my agent, and the Intellectual Freedom Committee of the American Library Association, the school system did the right thing. They didn't disinvite me, and as far as I know my book still lives on their shelves. They'd invited the parent to a meeting with teachers, librarians, and an administrator. "We dealt with her rationally and with understanding," the librarian said, "and I think it took the wind out of her sails. She was expecting a fight and went away disappointed."

I doubt it. I expect she equated rational understanding with weakness, and, after all, she'd won coverage in one of the most widely read newspapers in the country. And other parents who don't want their children's reading culled and censored didn't rise up. There was no thought of rallying them, and in the modern way they turned away.

Oddly, I met the parent who had tried to keep me out of town. She'd come to monitor my meeting with parents and seemed to write down every word I spoke. Impersonating a supportive parent in an audience swollen by the controversy, she didn't know I knew who she was. Even book banners who grant newspaper interviews appear to think they can preserve a kind of selective anonymity.

If the entire fundamentalist membership responded to the call from their pulpits, we'd have hardly a school program or library left. But this parent was a textbook case of the member who acts. She was new to the community and perhaps wasn't as widely known as she'd been where she'd come from, until she was quoted in the newspaper. One of her children was trembling on the brink of puberty and growing hard to handle and not making a very good adjustment to a new school. And not, truth to tell, much of a reader, according to a teacher.

I wasn't her focus, and she wouldn't have read more than the title of my book. Alerted, I happened to mention in my address to the parents that the book had been filmed for *The Wonderful World of Disney* and continues to be rerun on television. I met with the young people of that community and came away unscathed and with new readers, almost certainly including her son. Yet the damage had been done, a private tragedy to play out later. Because of his mother's actions a young boy at a vulnerable age had been set apart from his classmates and embarrassed. In the long run children will not forgive their parents that.

What can we do? Saying that it can't happen here doesn't work, though it's still being tried. Neither does our present purely defensive stance and our hope to promote books during the interludes of uneasy peace between the censorship wars.

Schools and libraries now have orderly processes by which challenged books can be defended. This comes as a surprise to some censors who didn't know and whose handlers hadn't told them. Many believe that one threatening phone call will eliminate a book, and it's been known to happen. It's time to be far more public about our systems for protecting the right to read and our resolve in enforcing these systems. Trying to keep the challenge to a book quiet in the name of damage control is itself a kind of censorship.

Book banners appear to fall into two camps, those who use the media and those who want to maintain deep cover. For both kinds we need to go public and use the local media in our own cause. An article outlining the methods in place for defending books, run in the newspaper at the beginning of a school year perhaps, is better than silent waiting.

Like adolescents, censors will test whatever system they can, except their own. When it comes to a face-to-face meeting, there are limits to responding to the programmed with rational understanding. Censors have an agenda, but they haven't heard ours. Book and education people have some points to make. One is our concern about the power of television over the home lives of young people. Schools haven't yet developed the political will to send home to all parents helpful guidelines for the limiting of television for their children, despite the time it takes from their learning. But it's a valid point to bring up in talking with parents who seek control over schools and libraries because they have so little at home. They will tell us that they have total authority over their children's screen-time and content, particularly the content of video games, and that's our opportunity to display grave skepticism.

Discussing the content of books with people who don't read them has its limits too. We might better turn the conversation to the fear and worry that parents have for the children. It's lurking just beneath the surface or we wouldn't be meeting these parents at all. I hear about some of the censorship cases involving my books from local newspaper reporters wanting my reaction.

One reporter was surprised twice. The book under fire was that same supernatural comedy filmed with impunity by Disney. His other surprise was that the censoring parent was a high-school teacher, though not of English or reading.

But it turned out that she had a child in sixth grade. On the job every day she very likely saw a high school being run by the students, and the inevitable loosening of her control over her own child sent her in search of a scapegoat and an attempt to purify the environment.

Book censorship comes from redirected fear, and book banners aren't from happy homes. We need to encourage parents to ventilate their real concerns rather than dignifying their search for scapegoats. Deferring to people who have insulted the professionalism of librarians and teachers has already lost us ground and time.

Censors aren't future-oriented. They want power now. Pointing out to a parent of a child in the upper grades that there's more trouble ahead is only fair. A high-school reading curriculum worth its salt will include *Macbeth,* which opens with not one witch, but three. *Hamlet* opens upon the ghost of Hamlet's father. *Julius Caesar*'s cast includes a soothsayer. The classics are full of things that go bump in the night. It's important to point out even to people who've never read *Macbeth, Hamlet,* or *Julius Caesar* (and who don't know that *Romeo and Juliet* is a suicide story about two sexually active teenagers whose parents disapprove) that book banning may occupy more of their time than they'd planned to give it.

Mention of the classics slows some people down. In her column Schlafly calls for the return of the classics without mentioning their titles or content. But whether the book in question is a classic or a light recreational read, we need to voice our concern for the nonreader's future—and chances for college admission.

Above all we have to make clear that we know it isn't true when censors of the "occult" maintain, as they invariably do, that they are acting independently or in a local group of other parents united solely by their concern. If they were acting on their own they'd come up with more original titles.

We have to use aggressive, public new ways to point out to people hungry for power that we aren't powerless. Those with sectarian motivation attend churches where they're in an absolute majority because all dissent is silenced. This can give them a distorted view of a world where they are still a minority.

As a result, when we meet, it shouldn't be one-on-one. They need to see librarians and teachers and administrators grouped, united, and ready. The lack of firm handling means only that we'll meet them again. Before I'd left that picture-perfect suburb, the censoring parent was already turning her attention to a junior-high science textbook with a sex education chapter.

We need strong response and all the high profile airing we can give this problem, because censors are beyond our attempts to reason together. In his article Donald Gallo says:

> In their fear for what might be damaging to their children, would-be censors seem to look at books from skewed perspectives. Where they see death, harsh words and inappropriate role models in Robert Cormier's short story "In the Heat," other readers—teenagers and adults—see the tender

love between fathers and sons and the comfort that love can bring during the painful process of coping with the death of a loved one. If people see only the pain and a few harsh words but miss the compassion, beauty, and sensitivity of the relationships in that story, then I wonder what kind of parents they really are—how sensitive, how understanding, how compassionate—and how much they really care about their children.

The day was destined to come when my files and my author-visit itinerary filled to overflowing with horror stories on the censorship subject. It was a battle fought and won and lost over the heads of the very people we wrote for.

I thought it was time to write a book asking the young themselves where they stood on the censorship wars. It wasn't ever to be an easy task; most of the young think *not* reading means they're winning. But too many real-life encounters, too many visits to frightened schools pushed me over the edge.

I was emboldened by Right to Read programs in schools and libraries, by the celebration of banned books many strong librarians conducted in the showcases and bulletin boards of their own libraries.

Since I didn't think the young would read nonfiction on the topic, I decided on a novel. A family story, as all our stories are. A story about a family who moves to the suburbs for the usual reason, not to face up to life's problems, but to avoid them:

We used to live out in the western suburbs. But when Diana and I were in sixth grade, the junior high out there had a

couple of knife fights that made news. The gangs were moving in, so we moved out.

It's a story about a boy just starting high school, wanting to be
on the team, wanting to meet the girl. And he does meet her, a
lovely girl. But she's been professionally programmed by a religious leader with political aspirations. She's easy prey because
she doesn't come from nearly as happy a family as the boy does:

> She turned to me, and it was Laurel, except without the
> careful smile. "Satan is everywhere, and his followers are
> here. In grade school it's all those hideous Halloween deco-
> rations that make little children love evil. That's what turns
> them into the kind of people you and I go to school with
> every day. Don't you know the devil and his workers are in
> that high school? Are you that blind?"

The novel is called *The Last Safe Place on Earth,* because there
isn't one.

The writer has to play all the parts, of course, even Laurel's. We
have to inhabit other people's skins and search perfect strangers
to find out who they are. In long nights after dark days, we even
wonder what's truly in the hearts and minds of our fellow adults
who want to purify their communities, and rid them of us:

> *What are you trying to tell me*
> *That I'm afraid to hear?*
> *What is the witchcraft in your words*
> *That strikes my soul with fear?*

Why are you trying to tell me
       Of the dangers I have to face
When I am hoping to live content,
       Safe in the smallest place?

Why are you telling my children
       Truths I don't want them to know?
If they learn too much, they'll leave me,
       And I don't want them to go.

What are those books on the library shelves?
       I don't read them, so I'm not sure,
But how do I know they aren't evil,
       Part of the devil's lure?

I don't need your words from the world
       Or how reading can set me free.
I'm doing fine, just as I am . . .

I wonder what's on TV?

CHAPTER TWELVE

In *Remembering the Good Times* Buck says:

> I was beginning to develop, at least physically, but nothing
> seemed to be the right size. Every morning I woke up, I had
> to check me out to see who was there. Some mornings I was a
> kid. Some mornings I was a maniac. Some mornings I didn't
> wake up at all; I just sleepwalked through the day.

In hindsight it seems inevitable, an American inevitability,
that any group of people this vulnerable would merit and elicit
a literature of their own. It follows in the longest thematic tradition of the American novel: coming of age in a country coming
of age.

It's said that through their literature, the English *invented* childhood. There was that eighteenth-century bookseller John Newbery, who self-published *Mother Goose's Nursery Rhymes*. And Dickens fathered Little Dorrit, Oliver Twist, David Copperfield, Pip and Estella. There was the English school story, once there were enough readers who went to school: *Tom Brown's School Days* by Thomas Hughes, Kipling's *Stalky & Co.,* Angela Brazil's *The Fortunes of Philippa*. There were Alice in Wonderland and Peter Rabbit.

The English may have invented childhood, but we invented adolescence. The first real American novel is *The Adventures of Huckleberry Finn,* about a boy who's no longer quite a child, if he ever was one. An American writer from Indianapolis, Booth Tarkington, discovered twentieth-century adolescence because he wrote *Alice Adams,* about a girl who goes to a party when it would have been so much safer to stay at home.

A long dry spell followed, a decade of depression, another of war, when we couldn't afford adolescence. After all, adolescence is a disease of the affluent. Then five novels came out of nowhere, to change ever after our view of the young, of being young: Betty Smith's *A Tree Grows in Brooklyn,* Carson McCullers's *The Member of the Wedding,* John Knowles's *A Separate Peace,* William Golding's *Lord of the Flies,* and J. D. Salinger's *The Catcher in the Rye.*

They weren't, of course, "children's books." They were written for an adult readership, and so they were easier to write. But they cut through the sentimentality. Though they didn't issue their challenges directly to the young reader, they dignified the young character with the treatment and portrayal formerly reserved for the adult character. They were the books that the writers of my generation read when we were young and impressionable, and they left their mark. They gave us new directions, and that's what books are for.

Then one day in the depths of the 1960's, one of those events occurred that seemed to be out of all context. A high-school girl in Tulsa went home every afternoon from school to write her novel. Nobody yet understands how she did it. She called the novel *The Outsiders* and herself S. E. Hinton.

S. E. Hinton knew things you can't know in adolescence, or maybe ever. She knew even in her teens that a novel needs to be about the reader, not the writer. She'd evidently been spared the creative-writing course, the one that says: "Write from your experience; spill yourself on the page." She knew that writing is communication, not self-expression, that nobody in this world wants to read your diary, except your mother.

S. E. Hinton knew all about aesthetic distance. Though she was a girl, she wrote about boys. Like all writers she was a loner, but she wrote about people in groups.

There was the in crowd at her school, the overindulged smart set, whom she called "Socs." There was the underclass: black-leather-jacketed, statusless—"Greasers." There were also those shadowy figures she never mentioned, the unorganized onlookers like herself. Wisely, she wrote about the Greasers and identified them in the title. She must have read *Huckleberry Finn,* because she wrote with confidence about people her readers wouldn't want to sit next to in class.

Though S. E. Hinton was herself an adolescent, she knew the central quest of adolescence, the impossible dream of replacing your family with your friends. She wrote about a gang that could never be, one you want to join, a gang that provides a sense of family for its members.

Since it was a family freed of parents, the world of young readers beat a path to her door. The phenomenal success of *The Outsiders* alerted the publishing industry to the possibilities of novels for and about the young. It even elicited letters to *The New York Times*:

> "I feel that Miss Hinton is a cliché grabber, not a free thinker. . . . I feel that America has more responsibility to the people of the world than to think teenagers are to be looked up to or catered to. . . . I have three teenaged children, and they just don't know any people like those in your book."[1]

S. E. Hinton was a strange wunderkind whose time had come. She was first on the scene at that greatest revolution since our first one. Her book led to a flourishing body of books about young people parents thought their children didn't know.

All novels are about private life, and suddenly in the sixties, young people of fifteen and thirteen and eleven had more private life than did their own parents: more frightening freedoms, ominous options, decisions.

The great theme in the last third of the American twentieth century was to be the tribalizing of the young. When families fragmented as units and as lawgivers, schools crumbled at the same rate.

1. August 8, 1967.

These times called forth a new kind of book, because novels are never about people living easy lives in a coherent universe. Novels are the biographies of survivors.

It may have been a great irony that a literature that didn't trivialize young people's lives developed at just the historic juncture when most of them couldn't read it. But these novels rushed into a vacuum to raise questions asked by parents and teachers in the past, and to ask new questions.

Judy Blume's *Are You There God? It's Me, Margaret.* became an icon among young girls because it reassured them that the changes going on in their minds and bodies and emotions weren't pathological, and that they weren't alone. Judy Blume still takes some heat from mothers for making contact with their daughters just as they're losing it.

Paul Zindel wrote *The Pigman*. M. E. Kerr wrote *Dinky Hocker Shoots Smack!* Theodore Taylor wrote *The Cay*. Robert Newton Peck wrote *A Day No Pigs Would Die*. Katie Letcher Lyle wrote *I Will Go Barefoot All Summer for You*. John Donovan wrote *I'll Get There, It Better Be Worth the Trip*. Alice Childress wrote *A Hero Ain't Nothin' but a Sandwich*, and somebody wrote *Go Ask Alice*.

Robert Cormier wrote *The Chocolate War*, a novel that will be read a hundred years from now because it chronicles that most important moment in American history, the time when the balance tipped and power passed from adults to children. It introduces the young authority figure who rises up when adults are no longer in charge, when teachers must defer to students in order to keep their jobs. It reinterprets *Lord of the Flies*.

Lord of the Flies is too easy. It's about British schoolboys on a distant island. *The Chocolate War* is about the school the reader is attending.

In 1975 Robert Cormier's book went through three printings in the first year of its paperback publication. It was a heaven-sent compensation that the technology of the paperback had coincided historically with the technology of television, though the battle was never to be equal. While Judy Blume's books didn't win unqualified backing from librarians, she went on to glory in the paperback bookstore, at the mall. Teens and preteens who never set foot in a library became book buyers. Their custom was especially brisk in bookstores that had the wit to shelve the young-adult books as far as possible from the children's books.

Librarians who perceived that we reached for readers at just the age when they are traditionally lost to reading almost singlehandedly supported young-adult books in hardback. The classroom teacher, even the desperate junior-high/middle-school teacher, was more reluctant.

We authors were alive, for one thing, and so we couldn't be classics. We weren't in the public domain either, and so the textbook anthologies were slow to excerpt us, though the time came. We made slow and spotty progress into the classroom, chiefly because teachers didn't have college notes on us. But the day came when some of the books we'd written for the leisure time of young readers were being introduced and discussed in classes. After all, our themes reflected the themes of more traditional readings and reinterpreted them in more immediate ways, harder for the young to call irrelevant.

Still, we remained a mysterious, almost underground

movement. Even our name was askew. We weren't writing for "Y.A.s"—young adults, who are people making their own living, and beds. We write for a far different group, the "P.L.s"—the pubescent literate.

Our readers don't read reviews, and adults who've never read us confuse us with the Hardy Boys and series romances and docudramas about unwed mothers. Our varieties of approach are various enough to baffle too.

We reach for readers through comedy and tragedy, fantasy and science fiction, intergenerational family life and school stories. We draw our themes from our readers' new patterns and from the oldest strains of storytelling. Robert Lipsyte, Chris Crutcher, Terry Davis follow John Tunis in putting sports stories to new uses. Robin Brancato's *Winning* goes further still. Walter Dean Myers's *Fallen Angels,* Peter Dickinson's *AK,* and Gary Paulsen's *Soldier's Heart* look again at war as a rite of passage. We've developed stylists: M. E. Kerr, Francesca Lia Block, and such a poet as Sonya Sones, in her *Stop Pretending.*

In their need for economy and proving-not-preaching, and in their use of the symbolic movement, some of our books grew more subtle than adult fare and invariably better paced. Some of them, as in any field, weren't worth the paper they were printed on. Whole forests fell in vain.

Through it all we pretty well retained a kind of productive privacy. Judy Blume and S. E. Hinton virtually alone broke the surface of public awareness. Judy Blume's books continue to be promoted by controversy. S. E. Hinton's have had high-image second lives as Hollywood films. But most of us preserved our anonymity, whether we wanted it or not. It's a field in which your books can sell a million copies and some of your own friends have no idea what you do for a living.

And what is a young-adult book? Though we're writing for the children of our first readers, the field is still evolving. But some of its traits have emerged.

A young-adult novel is, first of all, a novel. It isn't real life with the names changed, though it receives exaggerated attention when its central issue can be categorized in some nonliterary way: rape, running away, incest, drug abuse, gang warfare. But few young-adult novels are single-problem stories. Their preoccupation is with human relationships and portrayals rather than sociology.

A young-adult novel is a novel about how to read a novel. The shape of the novel is there in its arresting opening scene, its rising action, the moment of truth to be acted upon. It's an essentially traditional form for a readership less receptive to innovation than adult English majors.

It's a celebration of the individual, sharpened for readers at a time of life and history when the young individual is under particular fire and needs encouragement well beyond the needs of most adult readers, who know who they and their friends are.

It's the story of a step that one young character takes nearer to maturity. Now that adolescence has lost much of its purpose as a preparation for adulthood, the young-adult novel portrays a young character moving ahead regardless.

The young-adult novel provides an alternative. The main character is going to adopt a course of action that the reader may accept, but wouldn't have initiated. In one kind of book the character, symbolically, may have a fantastic or supernatural skill. In another the character may be acting on a personal decision by walking away from the peer-group establishment or acting in family life in ways the reader wouldn't, or hadn't thought of.

Like all novels, the young-adult novel has to entertain before it can do anything else. A novel must entertain on every page, but a young-adult novel needs to annoy on three. To tell the readers what they want to hear and nothing more replicates television and grade inflation. The fact that our main characters act upon the epiphany of a new awareness sends them in directions that often unnerve readers. And we don't tie our concluding scenes in the neat bows our readers prefer. As essentially moral tracts, young-adult novels introduce elements the readers weren't looking for. They are halfway through the book when they discover the central issue in M. E. Kerr's *Night Kites*.

In depicting reality our books are often on a collision course with our readers' most deeply felt beliefs: that they cannot die, or be infected with sexually transmitted diseases, or get pregnant unless they want to, or become addicted to anything. Our books regularly challenge their conviction that the rules don't apply to them. There are limits to the amount of reality the novel form can encompass. Young-adult novels test the boundaries.

This exploration of the gray area between word and deed leads to the subtext of all our books: the responsibility for the consequences of actions.

A young-adult novel is a shot fired just over the heads of the readers. The protagonist will be older than the readers. The diction of the novel won't be a controlled vocabulary drawn from a grade-level list. The novel must reach readers where they are, but it dares never talk down to them or leave them where it finds them. It can't speak as blandly as the textbook or with the repetition of television.

And it's a story that ends not with happily ever after, but at a new beginning, with the sense of a lot of life yet to be lived. Having taken the step dramatized in the novel, the young character as role model—flawed but functioning—is better prepared to move ahead. They are Frankie Adamses of both sexes who rise and walk.

Novels are questions, not answers. Our novels are adults in disguise, trying to make contact with young readers who have disguises of their own. There is this passage in Gary Paulsen's *Dogsong:*

> "Father, something is bothering me."
>
> He replied around the meat. "I know. I have seen it."
>
> "But I don't know what it is."
>
> "I know that, too. It is part that you are fourteen and have thirteen winters and there are things that happen then which are hard to understand. But the other part that is bothering you I cannot say because I lack knowledge. You must get help from some other place. . . . I think you should go and talk to Oogruk. He is old and sometimes wise and he also tells good stories."

Language is negotiation. It's what humanity devised after the brawl outside the cave. Our kind of books for young readers came along somewhat later. The present moment in history always looks more complicated and morally ambiguous than all previous eras. Our books are exercises in language that appear in a time when young people are losing their language, are less well-spoken than their own parents, than the very television they watch.

Language is negotiation, and the impetus to learn it is the need for negotiating, even early in life: negotiating with a teacher in the name of academic success, or survival, negotiating with Dad for the keys to his car. We write for a generation who have needed language less to get what they want from adults, who in their dealings with one another have reason to suspect that the pen is no longer mightier than the sword.

We make brief forays behind their defenses and then tell them stories about themselves. In books that we write one word at a time, we lure them into a world of words. We cannot make adolescent readers out of adolescent illiterates. If you have been coming to school for seven years without having to read, you've whipped the system and are lost to us all. Instead, our books give assurances and alternatives to young readers, who are the only future we have.

The years and the books roll on. Vintage clothing shops fill up with the antique finery of the early 1990's, and it occurs to me that I have neckties older than my readers. As the old century ebbed, we were being assured by many a slick salesman that the electronic library, the computerized classroom, the mighty microchip would transform education as we know it, would even convert the child who doesn't want to learn, could even trick a child into learning, and even rewriting.

We'd forgotten that if the young could learn more literacy from screens and machines than from living elders with books in their hands, it would all have happened forty years before with something called "audio-visual aids." Schools turned away from our books because they were teaching now to standardized literacy tests that would raise literacy levels, but won't.

Empires rose and fell: Russia, dot-com, the Boy Scouts, whole language. On the suburban skyline Barnes & Noble began to bulk bigger than the high-school gym. Harry Potter became the first juvenile hero most parents have heard of since the Hardy Boys.

A century turned. The old one ended early on an April morning in 1999 with a burst of gunfire in a suburban high school called with odd poetry: Columbine.

While the faculty retrained, marching off to many a weary computer clinic to learn how to be Charlottes in somebody's world-wide web, it's harder to say where the young went. Their parents had lived at the top of the barricades and their lungs. The offspring, deeply ensconced in inherited freedoms, grew ominously absent, with dwindling ties to adults as they approached adulthood.

Senior year in high school virtually vanished. Over-subscribed private schools ghettoized communities that had once been united by public schools. The unfallen Berlin wall dividing the gifted from the remedial in every school foretold a twenty-first century more fragmented and status-conscious than the twentieth.

Schools struggled for balance, their unspoken motto carved invisibly above the door:

ANNOY NO STUDENT,
ALERT NO PARENT

The music, the electronics, the clothing industries continued to know just where to find this new generation, but their parents seemed not to know where to look, and some weren't looking. A woman I know well said of her fourteen-year-old, "I never go near school now. I already know more about my child than I want to."

Yet I still get letters from them, letters confounding, delighting, perplexing. For a generation as enigmatic as this one, carrying on a correspondence can lead some of them to full disclosure, as in this pair of examples, one from a boy, the other from a girl:

I have an obsessive compulsive disorder, and I have to cope with a crazy sister, a tattletale, and my divorced parents. I think that a year of that life could be made into a comedy.

and

School is harder. I find myself making more mistakes and most of them can't really be fixed. I have to be careful about my actions because I'm with people that I will be near for the next six years.

And those people she has to be careful about aren't teachers.

After "How did you get your start?" and "Where do you get your ideas?" a mysterious number of letters ask a third question: "How much longer are you going to write?"

I'm stumped by the motive behind that question, and maybe I don't want to know. But its only answer is another question: How much longer am I going to live?

Writers don't retire. Like teaching, writing is something less than a profession, but more than a job. When you aren't teaching, you're thinking about teaching. When you're not writing, you're thinking about writing.

We writers don't retire. We just watch our backlists fall off.

So, How Much Longer Are You Going to Write?

As long as the letters keep coming, providing grins and the occasional tear. As long as my colleagues keep writing books that I admire and learn from, and wish I'd written. As long as coming of age continues to be so much harder than anything I can remember. As long as I can eavesdrop on other people's lives and stick my nose into their personal business, and call it "research." As long as I can.

Once years ago in a flippant and vainglorious mood after answering too many letters at a single sitting, I answered, "I'm going to keep writing until I win a Newbery medal," never dreaming . . .

CHAPTER THIRTEEN

At the end of 2000, young readers and their writers suffered a personal loss, the death of Robert Cormier. While his seminal *The Chocolate War* hadn't aged a minute in twenty-five years, his subsequent work retained an emotional involvement with the young, a literature to plumb their dark places. In the following year, his brief, posthumous novel, *The Rag and Bone Shop,* would provide a fitting footnote to his career.

In Michael Cart's *Booklist*[1] remembrance, he wrote this:

> I believe it is because of Robert Cormier that we can dignify the [young-adult] genre with that very word literature.

1. December 15, 2000.

Consider his courage in being the first to demonstrate—in *The Chocolate War*—that not every young-adult novel must have a happy ending opened enormous thematic possibilities for writers who would follow in his wake.

Consider, too, that he was a master of complex, multi-dimensional characterization, and he invited his readers to speculate about the role played, respectively, by free will and determinism in the lives of his characters.

Free will and determinism, heady stuff for young people who have reached their teens without ever having to read a book. But perhaps Robert Cormier's true legacy is that he didn't write down to anybody, a lesson to us all.

His books set standards through a time when schools could only make compromises. He was deaf to those who wanted to know the grade reading level of his books. He was deaf to "age-appropriateness." But he could hear the human heart, and his work lives on in books not yet written.

He has left us, in *The Chocolate War,* an iconic figure in fiction and fact, the adolescent and now the grade school peer-group leader who rose out of the 1970's, that seductive and punitive figure that teachers all these years later can identify as the most politically powerful, and popular, person at school.

A new century broke over us, and we found we'd moved from post-revolutionary to post-modern. E-mail indemnified the rough draft and struck a mortal blow to paragraphing. The video game, a violent virtual reality, eliminated the parent who paid for it.

Happily, American books for the young greeted a new century with a whole spectrum of worthy offerings, from picture books to coming-of-age novels. Never had such a range of talent, graphic and linear, shared their gifts with the young.

A clutch of young-adult novels appeared to mark and remark upon thirty years of a self-directed youth culture. One of them was Jerry Spinelli's *Stargirl,* a parable about adolescent conformity and one magical girl who makes a change in those around her. It's too beautifully written not to quote from:

> In the Sonoran Desert there are ponds. You could be standing in the middle of one and not know it, because the ponds are usually dry. Nor would you know that inches below your feet, frogs are sleeping, their heartbeats down to once or twice per minute. They lie dormant and waiting, these mud frogs, for without water their lives are incomplete, they are not fully themselves. For many months they sleep like this within the earth. And then the rain comes. And a hundred pairs of eyes pop out of the mud, and at night a hundred voices call across the moonlit water.
>
> It was wonderful to see, wonderful to be in the middle of: we mud frogs awakening all around. We were awash in tiny attentions. Small gestures, words, empathies thought to be extinct came to life. For years the strangers among us had passed sullenly in the hallways; now we looked, we nodded, we smiled. If someone got an *A,* others celebrated, too. If someone sprained an ankle, others felt the pain. We discovered the color of each other's eyes.[1]

1. Knopf, 2000.

A stirring novel, written by someone who may have read Shirley Jackson's story "The Lottery" when he was young and impressionable—because nobody but a reader ever became a writer.

Other new novels included Laurie Halse Anderson's *Speak,* Alex Flinn's *Breathing Underwater,* Sarah Dessen's *Dreamland,* Patricia McCormick's *Cut,* Chris Crutcher's *Whale Talk,* Walter Dean Myers's *Monster,* Sara Ryan's *Empress of the World.*

They're novels to remind us of that first wave that raised questions all those years ago. *Speak* recalls—even restates—*Are You in the House Alone? Whale Talk* remembers Crutcher's own first novel, *Running Loose.* It replays Hinton's *The Outsiders* with a counter-culture gang that wears Speedos instead of black leather. Sara Ryan's *Empress of the World* makes even *USA Today*[1] recall John Donovan's 1969 *I'll Get There, It Better Be Worth the Trip.* Critic Patty Campbell calls *Monster* "a groundbreaker to rival *The Chocolate War* and even *Catcher in the Rye.*"

These page-turners powerfully documented the foreign country adolescence has become in three decades of self rule. None of them repeated the breathiness of *Go Ask Alice.* In Dessen's *Dreamland,* Caitlin falls for Rogerson at the moment she sees him dealing drugs at a party. Hers is no moral dilemma; her only anxiety is to hide from her parents the bruises Rogerson inflicts upon her. Concealing from parents her deepening drug addiction is easier still. The substance abuse and sexual activity that were once the parents' political acts of righteous rebellion are givens now.

1. June 28, 2001.

These new novels composed an important group portrait of modern parents and teachers, the adults tentatively on the sidelines of their young people's lives.

In *Speak,* a rape victim appears never to share the news with her parents. Her all-consuming problem is peer-group disapproval because she's actually reported the crime.

In *Dreamland,* parents who locate a runaway older daughter never consider bringing her home. They are modern middle-class parents terrified of losing children they have long since lost.

Walter Dean Myers's *Monster* resonates with the sights and sounds of jailed male teenagers who now form a separate, immured society within our own: a prep school for their adult, twenty-first century lives. All the while, the monster's caring, helpless parents are on the far side of a barred window from the son they love.

These novels were invaluable reflections of how we live now. As proof that the young-adult genre was alive and well, books on uncomfortable subjects continued to draw fire.

The *USA Today* article that dealt with Sara Ryan's *Empress of the World* and Alex Sanchez's *Rainbow Boys* is headlined "Innocence and Ignorance: Coming of Age Books Give a Forthright Portrayal of Growing Up Gay."

Young-adult stories now treating homosexual teenagers as teenagers recall the very roots of young adult, when novels first began to take adolescent characters as seriously as if they were adults.

USA Today brought out big guns in our field to defend the books: Michael Cart, Roger Sutton, Pat Scales, and the editors of the two novels, Sharyn November and David Gale. But how eerie that in these latter days, books humanizing young gay characters need justification. Here again, books reflecting the daily lives of schools and students, books that edge near the real even when that reality can be labeled multicultural, are controversial as nothing on a screen can be.

Even after a decade of heavily publicized gay-bashing, of Laramie, Wyoming, and the continuing assaults upon designated victims by athletic teams, the Taliban of many schools, an article on gay-themed books had to give space to a concerned parent who runs a website called Parents Against Bad Books in Schools that posts excerpts from *Baby Be-Bop* by Francesca Lia Block.

We were reminded again of how little progress we've made in humanity and tolerance in a time when the young have been free to create their own tribal rules while their defeated parents go sulking in search of scapegoats.

I was reading that article on a long drive from the Idaho Falls airport. The driver was a science teacher in a Montana town of a hundred people. I asked him if he taught about AIDS in his science classes. He said he did.

"But all your students believe they are immune to AIDS, don't they?" I said.

He answered quietly, "They believe they're immune to everything."

More work for the novelist, to be on the record for young readers who might be willing to hear a message that all around them are deaf to.

My own, less edgy turn-of-the-century novel on a contemporary issue is *Strays Like Us*. Its beginning, heavy with omens, finds twelve-year-old Molly having to start seventh grade in a new place:

> I was on the bed, and my school clothes were hanging where I could see them. Had I been wearing a blindfold when I picked them? I didn't know which to wear on the first day or what went with what. I didn't care about clothes, but I didn't want to stand out. I'd as soon wear my Six Flags T-shirt and the raggedy shorts I'd lived in all summer. But a voice inside me said I better not. I was twelve, so I was beginning to hear little voices inside me.

Her vagrant mother is in de-tox, and a social worker has delivered Molly to her nearest known relative, a stranger: elderly, childless Great-Aunt Fay. Like thousands of others, the children of a misfiring parental generation, Molly is a foster child.

Can she find community and family where the print-outs of the welfare state place her? Yes, she can because a novel adds hope to reality. Can she find "closure"? Possibly not, because a novel is not the psychiatrist's couch. But she can find a new beginning:

> I loved my mother, and she loved me. She loved me like a rag doll you drag around and then leave out in the rain. I still love her, but I live here.

Strays Like Us sprang straight from a school visit. I was once invited to a consolidated country school, and I looked forward to a rare encounter with farm kids and their rural point of view.

I was standing at the window of the school library that morning when the school buses drew up. Down their steps tumbled every urban stereotype you ever saw: black leather and rainbow hair, and bristling with hardware—just plain bristling, in fact.

"Who are *they*?" I asked the librarian beside me.

"They're children sent by their parents or the social worker back to extended family, mostly grandparents."

"How many?" I asked, amazed.

"Seventy percent of the school," she said. "But for them, we'd be closed now."

Then she said that thing that makes you write a novel: "And you know it doesn't work. The grandparents have problems of their own—aging, health, poverty. And besides . . . they'd already failed with the parents."

Part of the romance of writing is that the people who hand you your book ideas never know they're doing it.

I'd had my first glimpse of a vast, nomadic young population, adrift in search of home and family. I wondered how many I'd seen in earlier school visits without recognizing them. I wondered if I could write a story that might give them some identity, and dignity, because I wondered how welcome they were in the schools where they end up. We write in wonder, and because we wonder.

In two far less serious stabs at post-modernity I wrote a pair of computer-driven satires called *Lost in Cyberspace* and *The Great Interactive Dream Machine*—for the fun of slinging around terms from the barbaric new cyberspeak language. The dialogue is snappy and sassy, as well it might be since it's told through the eyes of two New York City Upper East Side private-school boys. Aaron is a computer whiz, meaning he can get into trouble at the keyboard that he can't get out of. His always-a-step-behind best friend, Josh, is computer illiterate and my own surrogate in the story.

But these yarns aren't as new as they're dressed up to look. In *Lost in Cyberspace* Aaron programs a computer to reorganize every cell in their bodies to send them back in time. However brilliant though, he's only in sixth grade, and his equation mis-fires. Every time they return from the past, they bring someone with them.

The sequel, *The Great Interactive Dream Machine,* is a more traditional tale still. Aaron comes up with a formula that causes his mainframe to grant wishes—three wishes. But nothing can run smoothly in a comedy. In this one the first wish the computer grants is the deepest desire of a French poodle. The second is the fondest wish of an elderly lady, and so it's about the past.

The past again.

While my colleagues were coming up with a new range of rough, ready, and readable contemporary novels that rushed in where no parent dared to tread, I began to drift back.

The new century found me approaching the age when the past is more vivid—and attractive—than the present. I'd suffered bouts of nostalgia before, as far back as *The Ghost Belonged to Me.* Researching in the library for a period story had been a good way to catch my breath between contemporary novels. In a way, it's easier to research the past than to nail the speech, the trends, the look of the present—and to wonder how long they'll last.

An opportunity came in a letter that Harry Mazer sent out to his writing colleagues in the fall of 1995. He asked us to write stories for an anthology he was assembling, a collection of gun stories. It was to become *Twelve Shots* from Delacorte Press.

Our careers hang on slender threads. Would Harry Mazer have considered a gun story collection a few months later in the aftermath of Columbine? Would a publisher have considered it?

Even at the time, I had to wonder how many librarians are members of the National Rifle Association. And I hadn't squeezed off a round myself since the rifle range at Fort Carson, Colorado, in January 1957.

Trying to envision the stories Harry would get, I thought a lot of them might be macho-menaced testosterone tales about how I shot a bear and it made a man out of me. I suspected seriousness and a given amount of blood in the streets. So just to give the collection some balance, I gave myself an assignment. I'd write a comic short story about a female character. A story set in the past, as it happened. I looked up from my desk, and there in the doorway stood Grandma Dowdel with a 12-gauge, double-barreled Winchester shotgun loose in her trigger-happy hand.

The story was "Shotgun Cheatham's Last Night Above Ground." I ran it past my editor, Cindy Kane. She thought there was a book in it, a gathering of short stories building to a novel.

It became *A Long Way from Chicago,* narrated by a boy named Joey, who along with his little sister, Mary Alice, is sent from Chicago to their grandma's remote farm town through the summers of the Great Depression. In each annual visit from

1929 to 1935 they see a different woman in their grandmother, though she never changes. She was, in fact, my retort to all those cloying portrayals of sweet little old ladies knitting by the fire in kiddies' picture books.

Grandma Dowdel is treetop tall, a local landmark, and popularly thought to be capable of anything. She walks a fine line with the law too, when she isn't making her own rules:

> "Grandma," I said, "is trapping fish legal in this state?"
>
> "If it was," she said, "we wouldn't have to be so quiet."
>
> "What's the fine?"
>
> "Nothin' if you don't get caught."

It takes Joe more than a few summers to begin to see that Grandma Dowdel's moral code transcends mere laws, and the men who enforce them. It takes him longer than that to learn that she's capable of anything, including irony. He's almost a man before he sees how much she loves him.

Grandma Dowdel took on extraordinary life. No character had lifted off the page as she did since Blossom Culp, to whom she is kin. *A Long Way from Chicago* became a National Book Award finalist in 1998, complete with a bronze medal to hang around the author's neck at the awards ceremony in New York.

It became the Newbery silver medalist from the American Library Association in 1999.

People were soon asking if Grandma Dowdel was a portrait of my own grandmother. Even librarians asked. Writers aren't given much credit for creativity. Did my own grandmother fire off both barrels of a shotgun in her front room? Did she trap fish from a boat stolen from the sheriff? No, actually, she didn't. When you're a writer, you can give yourself the grandmother you wish you'd had.

She isn't the first, or the last, of the strong, eccentric old folks stalking through my pages. Her immediate predecessor and prototype, though nobody had seemed to notice this, is Aunt Fay Moberly in *Strays Like Us*.

The setting for the story, though, like all my settings, is a real place. Significantly, it isn't my hometown. It's my father's hometown, a paradise lost to him on the battlefields of World War I. It's a farm town in Piatt County, Illinois, called Cerro Gordo, named by the men returning from the Mexican War of the 1840's, a town with open fields at the end of every randomly paved street.

Grandma Dowdel's house, the last one in town, is the house where my own grandmother lived, a tall carpenter-Gothic with lightning rods and snowball bushes crowding the bay window and a concrete walk down past the clothesline to the cob house and the privy. Stories for me are always what might have been in places that are.

When a book wins awards, the editor strongly suggests a sequel. Thus *A Year Down Yonder* began to be. With another Grandma Dowdel book due, I saw I'd made a grave error in a career full of them. I'd let Joey, of *A Long Way from Chicago*, grow up. He was in World War II, and so a sequel was out of the question.

Luckily, Joey's younger sister, Mary Alice, was waiting in the wings. She was destined to tell a different story, a novel to be called *A Year Down Yonder*. Joey had been awed by the power of a mighty grandmother, and perhaps of all women. Mary Alice finds in an unexpected place the role model for the rest of her life.

It begins for her during the Roosevelt recession of 1937 when she's fifteen. Her parents lose their Chicago home, and she has to go live with Grandma Dowdel for a year, a school year.

> As the train pulled out behind me, there came Grandma up the platform steps. My goodness, she was a big woman. I'd forgotten. And taller still with her spidery old umbrella held up to keep off the sun of high noon. A fan of white hair escaped the big bun on the back of her head. She drew nearer till she blotted out the day.
>
> You couldn't call her a welcoming woman, and there wasn't a hug in her. She didn't put out her arms, so I had nothing to run into.

The past is prologue, and a historical setting is a way of looking at the present. A comic novel about a girl looking for shelter sixty-five years ago is meant to ring more recent bells in the minds of young readers who very shortly now won't be able to remember the twentieth century.

And who is Grandma Dowdel? Since nobody but a reader ever became a writer, she marches in a long tradition. She is the American tall tale in a Lane Bryant dress. There's more than a bit of Paul Bunyan about her, and even a touch of the Native American trickster tradition.

And so is she multicultural? I'd like to think so. I never label her race, ethnicity, or origins, and heaven knows, she never tells. I'd like her to be the reader's grandmother, wherever in the wide world her village is. She was translated into Japanese, for example, by a translator badly baffled by the phrase "Let the door hit you where the dog bit you."

A Year Down Yonder won the Newbery gold medal for 2001, conferred at the Newbery Caldecott dinner in San Francisco.[1]

That was my opportunity to thank my writing colleagues for the inspiration of their work and friendship, a chance to thank Harry Mazer for sparking the short story that led to two books, an evening to remember Robert Cormier. And it was an opportunity to thank not one, but two editors who saw these books through, Cindy Kane and Lauri Hornik.

It was a time to recall that Grandma Dowdel is one of many in my army of the elderly. These ambulatory ancient monuments are there to offer wisdom and balance unavailable elsewhere. They're meant to be extended family for young suburban readers and for young readers in cement cities where the old fear the streets. Mainly, the old survivors are in my stories to embody that underlying message in all fiction: that in the long run you will be held responsible for the consequences of your actions. It's a truth that comedy tells, I believe, at least as well as tragedy.

An unexpected pleasure of Grandma Dowdel is the number of adults saying they were sharing her with their parents as well as with their children. All that research I did on depression-era America seemed to pay off with readers older than I who remembered that time. A cross-over book? My fingers are still crossed. All our books should cross over to adult readers. They

1. See *The Horn Book Magazine,* July/August 2001.

might just open up a line of communication between the generations. They might be just as good as the cell phone for keeping in touch, maybe better.

The older I get, the more opportunities I see in drawing that line between the very old and the very young: people just entering the world and people just leaving it, with that precious, informative moment of overlap.

The book that followed *A Year Down Yonder* was *Fair Weather*. Giving Grandma Dowdel and the Great Depression a well-earned rest, I created a new oldster, Granddad Fuller, and I went fishing in another stream, and century, for the setting.

To hear him tell it, Granddad Fuller is the last of the prairie pioneers:

> "When we was settlin' this part of the country," he said in his high croak, "all we had to eat with was a pocketknife for cutlery and a tin plate. That's all we had, and we were happy to have it. I don't recollect when I saw my first fork in this district."

But like all the old, he defies time. He's about to set off with his grandchildren, Lottie and Rosie and Buster, for the adventure of their lives, the World's Columbian Exposition, the Chicago world's fair of 1893.

They who have never seen a lightbulb will witness the White City Exposition blazing at midnight brighter than noon. They who've never traveled faster than a horse gallops will go on the train. They who have never seen a building taller than a silo will ride history's first Ferris wheel.

The great exposition began to fan out below us, and all the pavilions were like frosted wedding cakes. It was the White City on blue lagoons against the endless lake. Golden statues caught the last of the setting sun. Then like sudden morning the electric lights came on. If I could show you anything, I would show you that. The searchlight turned, and everything was washed in light like there could never be darkness again.

They find their futures at the fair . . . in a book, of course, where we hope all the young will look for their futures, and find them.

The future is the past repeating. *Fair Weather* is set at that moment of drama when the curtain rose on the new twentieth century. The fair was all about how electronic technology would solve everything. The book was published on September 10, 2001. I'm jarred now by its first line, though I wrote it myself:

It was the last day of our old lives, and we didn't even know it.

September 11 may well be remembered as the first day of the twenty-first century. On the weekend before, my sister and I breakfasted at the White House with President and Mrs. Bush in a gathering of writers: Patricia and Fredrick McKissack; David McCullough, the biographer of John Adams; Scott Turow; Mr. and Mrs. Walter Dean Myers; Natalie Babbitt; Katherine Paterson; Jon Scieszka, "The Stinky Cheese Man";

Doris Kearns Goodwin; Patricia MacLachlan, the creator of *Sarah, Plain and Tall*.

It was the first National Book Festival, organized by our first librarian First Lady. We moved from the White House to the lawn of the Capitol. There, readers of every taste and age, parents and their children, moved from tent to tent, hearing writers read from our work. Hundreds were expected; thousands came. It was the way the world should be. Three days later, that world came to an end.

In the aftermath of the attack upon our country, Mrs. Bush remained at her post—on radio, on television, on *Oprah*—urging us to read to our children, now more than ever, even if they think they're too old to be read to. "Let yours be the last voice they hear before they go to sleep," she said.

She is a woman who has met her moment. Her advice, of course, is for parents who live under the same roofs as their children. She refers to children who are home on a school night, who have bedtimes.

When life—history—makes us start over, some of us have to write verse, short verse, in an attempt to pull all the sprawling world upon a single page, if only to give ourselves someplace to stand. I had to:

September 11

We thought we'd outdistanced history—
Told our children it was nowhere near;
Even when history struck Columbine,
It didn't happen here.

We took down the maps in the classroom,
And when they were safely furled,
We told the young what they wanted to hear,
That they were immune from a menacing world.

But history isn't a folded-up map,
Or an unread textbook tome;
Now we know history's a fireman's child,
Waiting at home alone.

Knocked sideways by the attack, we said it was a wake-up call. What a good thing if it had awakened our schools that had long since fallen into the evasive tactics of never scarring their students with accurate grades and regarding Ritalin as a teaching tool.

Certainly the need arose for a new curriculum. The old one didn't work anymore, if it ever had.

September 11, 2001, dramatized the need for the rigorous study of geography, once we learned that geography is no defense against history. And the young need geography because they will live in the smallest worlds they can, and recognize no territory beyond their turf. Suddenly, we needed school libraries paved and papered with maps to make the point that the journey to the world begins in the library, not the gym.

All in a single day, we needed a whole new system of history study: sequential, victimless history and how it repeats—how people who have forgotten the past are condemned to repeat it.

We needed a revamped, required study of government, to

begin the slow, painstaking process of convincing the young that there are governments beyond their peer groups.

We needed foreign language as a requirement in this shrinking world, and Spanish, which is no longer a foreign language. Abruptly we could not afford the irony of beating the multicultural drum while simultaneously teaching foreign language to fewer and fewer students.

We needed a whole new curriculum for a new and challenging century. But to reintroduce the serious study of history and geography and government and foreign language—and English instead of "Language Arts"—would take courage.

It would mean lots more literacy and far fewer electives. It would mean limiting the gifted-and-talented program to the gifted and talented. It would mean schools returning to their only two legitimate functions: the teaching of non-elective literacy and delayed gratification.

It would take parents and teachers and administrators and librarians working together, free of fear of their children, for the first time in living memory.

It shows little sign of happening. A generation of parents and teachers—of us adults—who could turn away from the several lessons of Columbine even when it happened in a community just like ours, can deny anything.

More work for the writers. We've been spotting for survivors long before now, hoping to put that right book in the right young hand because we believe a book is the best invitation to the world.

A picture book for preschoolers is an invitation to the turning page, and the best defense we have against television as a baby-sitter.

A chapter book for grade-schoolers is the debut of the paragraph, and the paragraph is an endangered species now, all but exterminated by e-mail. The chapter book—by Beverly Cleary, Louis Sachar, Betsy Byars, Bruce Coville—is about how black letters on a white page can become full color. It's the best defense we have against the video game and its celebration of dismemberment and grotesque death as a popular art form.

A book for younger teens, a young-adult novel for the puberty people, lies at the heart of the matter, because puberty is that bleak interlude when we've always lost most young people to reading, even in far better days than these.

And a young-adult novel addressed to high-school readers, to adolescents, is on the great American theme: coming of age in a world made wrong. It's about taking that first faltering step onto the first rung of adult life—and always independently, because a novel celebrates the individual, not the mass movement.

The young-adult novel, that bridge to the adult world, is the best defense we have against the omnipotence of the peer group and its non-reading leader. In its anticipation of the future, the Y.A. novel is our best defense against the starting five on the varsity basketball team, who will never be this famous again.

"Words are the only thing which last forever," Winston Churchill once said. Somehow that truth seems truer now, here in the gray dawn of an uncertain new century. Books prepare the literate for change. Never have we needed the words within these books more, to comfort the isolated; to question the twin pillars of adolescence: conformity and entitlement; to weave plots; and to invite the imagination, we who believe that

A story is a doorway
> *That opens on a wider place;*
A story is a mirror
> *To reflect the reader's face.*

A story is a question
> *You hadn't thought to ponder;*
A story is a pathway,
> *Inviting you to wander.*

A story is a window,
A story is a key,
A story is a lighthouse,
Beaming out to sea.

A story's a beginning;
> *A story is an end;*
And in the story's middle,
> *You might just find a friend.*

FOR SHARING

SEVEN DO'S AND DON'T'S

Advice for parents who want their children to read

DON'T'S

1. Never say to yourself or to others "My child just isn't into reading, but has so many other interests." Your child won't get far with those other interests as a functional illiterate. There's a literature for every field: scientific, artistic, athletic, vocational, professional, parental. Successful people in those fields must have access to it.

2. Never imply by word or attitude that reading and writing (including letter writing) are woman's work.

3. Never tell your child or anyone else that your child is gifted. Outsiders will smile away your biased opinion, and you have reason to hope your child doesn't believe it either. An A on a report card today may mean either that your child is not being challenged, or that everybody is getting A's just for turning up. A's without homework are danger signals.

4. Never complain about a teacher or a school program if you don't personally know the school administration and faculty. If you've been sending your children off in the care of strangers throughout their school lives, you have no leverage when you appear at school—a stranger yourself—with a complaint.

5. Never worry about a book corrupting your child. Don't blame a book for giving the sex education you haven't gotten around to. Worry if your children aren't getting ideas from books. If your children aren't reading, they're at the mercy of the standards and whims of their peer group, standards to which you have less access than to what appears in print.

6. Never use a book as a scapegoat for your inability to control your children's television addiction, and never worry over the words in a book your children already knew before they could read or see regularly written on walls.

7. Never try to ban a book unless you want to help the author publicize it.

Do's

1. Give your preschool children literacy training. Don't worry that being able to read and write will leave them bored when they get to school. They may be bored either way.

2. Read aloud to children as much as you can, and don't stop even after they can read for themselves. Books are bonds between you and them.

3. Encourage and reward the memorizing of short passages. Spoken poetry emphasizes the rhythms of our language and strengthens both speech and writing.

4. Play vocabulary games with your children of all ages to increase their vocabularies and yours. If your children aren't communicating well with you, maybe they don't have any words.

5. Make sure there are maps in your house. Geography is no longer learned in schools, and young people don't read newspapers. Maps, as well as being eloquent employers of the written word in one of its most romantic modes, remind the young that they aren't the center of the world. They need a lot of reminding of that.

6. Make sure your children have library cards from their earliest years and feel at home in the part of the library especially for them. Give books as holiday gifts instead of toys. Toys are a poorer value and harder to share. Let your young equate gift-giving with reading. They probably already have all the toys they'll ever need.

7. Let your child observe you reading: books and magazines and newspapers that reflect your own tastes and interests. Independent reading is the badge of adulthood, of manhood and womanhood. The young are hungry for the advantages of maturity. Reading is one of them, and they can have it now, with your help.

TEN QUESTIONS TO ASK ABOUT A NOVEL

In a time when the written book report has gone the way of the diagramed sentence, the class discussion of a book remains the usual way of eliciting reader response. Most discussion leaders could use some new questions if only to discourage the "I liked it/didn't like it" reaction.

Herewith, ten questions to ask about a piece of fiction. Herewith, too, the ulterior motive in asking each question:

1. What would this story be like if the main character were of the opposite sex?

(Ulterior Motive): to approach the thinking of the author, who must decide what kind of protagonist or narrator will best embody or express the viewpoint. Could the protagonist of *The Member of the Wedding* be a boy instead of a girl? Could Jerry Renault in *The Chocolate War* be a female victim of a female gang? Certainly, though each book would seem different in many superficial ways. Such a question might even temporarily defuse the sexual polarization rampant in junior high.

2. Why is this story set where it is (not *what* is the setting)?

(Ulterior Motive): to point out the setting as an author's device to draw the reader into the action by means of recognizable trappings. The isolated setting of *Lord of the Flies* is a clear, if negative, example. But why is a soap opera almost always placed in an upper middle class suburban setting? Why do so few Y.A. novels occur in historic or exotic locales?

3. If you were to film this story, what characters would you eliminate if you couldn't use them all?

(Ulterior Motive): to contrast the human richness of a novel with the necessary simplification of a TV show. Confronted with the need to eliminate some of the characters who add texture, some readers may rise up in defense of their favorites.

4. Would you film this story in black and white or in color?

(Ulterior Motive): to consider *tone*. The initial reaction in this florid age is to opt for color in everything. But some young readers may remember the most chilling Dracula films are in black and white, perhaps in part because dark shadows are always darkest and black blood is more menacing than red.

5. How is the main character different from you?

(Ulterior Motive): to relent for once in our attempts to get the young readers to identify on their own limited terms. Protagonists regularly embody traits for the reader to aspire to. In Y.A. books, they typically have powers, insights, and surmountable drawbacks that readers will often respond to without possessing.

6. Why would or wouldn't this story make a good TV series?

(Ulterior Motive): to contrast the shaping of a book's sequential chapters in the larger shape of the plot to the episodes of a TV series that repeat narrowly but don't rise from their formula to a central conclusion.

7. What's one thing in this story that's happened to you?

(Ulterior Motive): to elicit an anecdotal response that draws the reader into the book. Y.A. novels typically deal in the shock of recognition in their depiction of highly realistic school, social, and personal situations. Science fiction and fantasy use very human situations to balance their more fabulous elements and to make room for the earthbound reader.

8. Reread the first paragraph of Chapter 1. What's in it that makes you read on?

(Ulterior Motive): to begin a book where the author must, in assessing the need for immediate involvement in an age not known for its patient attention span. An even more wistful motive: to suggest that young people include in their own writing immediately attractive devices for gaining the attention of the reader, if only the poor teacher.

9. If you had to design a new cover for this book, what would it look like?

(Ulterior Motive): to consider the often deceptive packaging of the book in this visual era, particularly the paperback cover, and to encourage a more skeptical eye among those who were being bombarded by packaging and commercial claims long before they could read.

10. What does the title tell you about the book? Does it tell the truth?

(Ulterior Motive): to remind the reader that the title may well be the most important words the author writes and to encourage their defenses against titles that titillate and oversell.

BOOKS BY RICHARD PECK

Novels for Young Adults

1972	Don't Look and It Won't Hurt
1973	Dreamland Lake
1973	Through a Brief Darkness
1974	Representing Super Doll
1975	The Ghost Belonged to Me
1976	Are You in the House Alone?
1977	Ghosts I Have Been
1978	Father Figure
1979	Secrets of the Shopping Mall
1981	Close Enough to Touch
1983	The Dreadful Future of Blossom Culp
1985	Remembering the Good Times
1986	Blossom Culp and the Sleep of Death
1987	Princess Ashley
1988	Those Summer Girls I Never Met
1989	Voices After Midnight
1991	Unfinished Portrait of Jessica
1993	Bel-Air Bambi and the Mall Rats
1995	The Last Safe Place on Earth
1995	Lost in Cyberspace
1996	The Great Interactive Dream Machine
1998	Strays Like Us
1998	A Long Way from Chicago
1999	Amanda/Miranda
2000	A Year Down Yonder
2001	Fair Weather

Novels for Adults

1980	Amanda/Miranda
1981	New York Time
1983	This Family of Women
1998	London Holiday

Picture Book

1977	Monster Night at Grandma's House (Illustrated by Don Freeman)

Autobiography

1991	Anonymously Yours

OTHER BOOKS MENTIONED IN THIS VOLUME

Laurie Halse Anderson	*Speak*
Francesca Lia Block	*Baby Be-Bop*
Judy Blume	*Are You There God? It's Me, Margaret.*
	Forever
	Tiger Eyes
Robin Brancato	*Winning*
Angela Brazil	*The Fortunes of Philippa*
Bruce Brooks	*The Moves Make the Man*
Michael Cart (ed.)	*Love and Sex: Ten Stories of Truth*
Alice Childress	*A Hero Ain't Nothin' but a Sandwich*
Pam Conrad	*Taking the Ferry Home*
Robert Cormier	*The Chocolate War*
	The Rag and Bone Shop
	We All Fall Down
Chris Crutcher	*Running Loose*
	Whale Talk
Sarah Dessen	*Dreamland*
Peter Dickinson	*AK*
John Donovan	*I'll Get There, It Better Be Worth the Trip*
Lois Duncan	*Killing Mr. Griffin*
Louise Fitzhugh	*Nobody's Family Is Going to Change*
Alex Flinn	*Breathing Underwater*
Donald R. Gallo (ed.)	*Connections*
	Sixteen
William Golding	*Lord of the Flies*
Hannah Green	*I Never Promised You a Rose Garden*
Bette Greene	*Summer of My German Soldier*
Judith Guest	*Ordinary People*
Rosa Guy	*The Music of Summer*
S. E. Hinton	*The Outsiders*
	Tex
Will Hobbs	*Downriver*
Isabelle Holland	*Of Love and Death and Other Journeys*
Thomas Hughes	*Tom Brown's School Days*
Scott Johnson	*One of the Boys*
M. E. Kerr	*Dinky Hocker Shoots Smack!*
	Gentlehands
	Night Kites
	The Son of Someone Famous

Rudyard Kipling	*Stalky & Co.*
John Knowles	*A Separate Peace*
Ron Koertge	*The Arizona Kid*
Harper Lee	*To Kill a Mockingbird*
Katie Letcher Lyle	*I Will Go Barefoot All Summer for You*
Harry Mazer (ed.)	*Twelve Shots*
Patricia McCormick	*Cut*
Carson McCullers	*The Member of the Wedding*
Patricia MacLachlan	*Sarah, Plain and Tall*
Walter Dean Myers	*Fallen Angels*
	Monster
Phyllis Reynolds Naylor	*All but Alice*
Katherine Paterson	*Jacob Have I Loved*
Gary Paulsen	*Dogsong*
	The Haymeadow
	Soldier's Heart
Robert Newton Peck	*A Day No Pigs Would Die*
Sara Ryan	*Empress of the World*
J. D. Salinger	*The Catcher in the Rye*
Graham Salisbury	*Blue Skin of the Sea*
Alex Sanchez	*Rainbow Boys*
Betty Smith	*A Tree Grows in Brooklyn*
Sonya Sones	*Stop Pretending*
Jerry Spinelli	*Stargirl*
Marc Talbert	*The Purple Heart*
Booth Tarkington	*Alice Adams*
Mildred Taylor	*Roll of Thunder, Hear My Cry*
Theodore Taylor	*The Cay*
Terry Trueman	*Stuck in Neutral*
Mark Twain	*The Adventures of Huckleberry Finn*
Cynthia Voigt	*Dicey's Song*
	Homecoming
Lawrence Yep	*Child of the Owl*
Paul Zindel	*The Effect of Gamma Rays on Man-in-the-Moon Marigolds*
	The Pigman
Anonymous	*Go Ask Alice*